WOMEN
OF
STEEL

Female Blue-Collar Workers in
the Basic Steel Industry

Kay Deaux and
Joseph C. Ullman

Library of Congress Cataloging in Publication Data

Deaux, Kay.
    Women of steel.

    Bibliography: p.
    Includes index.
    1. Women iron and steel workers—United States.
I. Ullman, Joseph C. II. Title.
HD6073.I52U63   1983   331.4'869142'0973   83-2434
ISBN 0-03-062008-2

Published in 1983 by Praeger Publishers
CBS Educational and Professional Publishing
A Division of CBS, Inc.
521 Fifth Avenue, New York, New York 10175 U.S.A.

456789 052 98765432
Printed in the United States of America
on acid-free paper.

Acknowledgements

The project reported in this volume could not have been accomplished without the aid of a great many people. The research itself was supported by the Employment and Training Division of the U.S. Department of Labor. Although the opinions expressed within this book do not necessarily reflect the views of that agency, their financial assistance to the project was essential to its conduct.

In conducting the research, we were assisted by Walt Duhaime, Magid Mazen, Judy Peterson, and especially by Valerie Steffen. Without their contributions and work through all phases of the project, we could not have completed the task. Patricia McDougall performed many editorial chores, made a substantial contribution to the preparation of Chapter 3, and was generally helpful in preparing the manuscript.

Numerous colleagues have read sections of the book and have offered their opinions and expertise. For these contributions, we thank Laurie Lewis, Brenda Major, Bruce Meglino, and Linda Putnam. The entire manuscript was read by Vernon Briggs, Irene Diamond, and Barbara Gutek, and their suggestions have improved the volume in many ways. We also appreciate the enthusiastic support of our editor, George Zimmar.

Finally, and perhaps above all, we are grateful to the women and men of steel. Production workers, craft workers, supervisors and management personnel—members of each of these groups have shared their time, resources, and views with us, allowing us to report their story in this book.

Contents

Introduction

Rosie keeps a sharp lookout for sabotage
Sitting up there on the fuselage.
That little frail can do,
More than a man can do,
Rosie, the riveter.
Rosie's got a boyfriend, Charlie;
Charlie, he's a marine.
Rosie is protecting Charlie
Working overtime on the riveting machine.

Rosie the Riveters gained fame during World War II as thousands of women entered the mills, the shipyards, and other sites of heavy industry. What was remarkable about this movement was not that women were working—many of these women, in fact, had worked for years in other jobs. What was new was the type of job. With the call for men to enter the armed forces, blue-collar jobs in heavy industry were available, and demanded to be filled if the war effort was to be successful. If able-bodied men were not available, then women would have to fill the void. And women did.

After the war, women were moved out of these jobs to make room for the returning male soldiers. In many cases, these moves were not voluntary. Women who had experienced the higher wages of traditionally male jobs were not always happy to return to the lower wages of secretarial, clerical, and service jobs. Furthermore, many women had found that they enjoyed the work that the factories and mills offered. The decrease in women holding blue-collar jobs was sudden, but not permanent. In recent years, increasing numbers of women have entered blue-collar work in general, and heavy industry in particular. It is with some of these women—women working in the basic steel industry—that this book is concerned.

Many books and articles have been written in recent years about the employment of women. Statistics showing that the number and percentage of women in paid employment is steadily increasing have provided the impetus for many of these commentaries. Yet, to a large extent, the subject of these writings has been a narrow one. Professional women have been spotlighted most frequently. Women in management have been discussed by numerous writers (e.g., Hennig & Jardim, 1976; Gordon & Strober, 1975; Kanter, 1977). Professors, doctors, and lawyers have also been frequent subjects of the academic writer, perhaps because similarity between investigator and subject makes that territory more comfortable. However, the bulk of women, like the bulk of men, do not hold professional jobs. Many women hold such "pink-collar" jobs as waitress, beautician, and sales worker (Howe, 1977). Many others hold clerical and secretarial jobs, typically the lowest paid of white-collar jobs. And fewer, but increasing numbers, hold blue-collar jobs.

Our interest lies with these blue-collar women. More specifically, we are interested in women who are working in traditionally male settings—the women to whom Walshok (1981) has referred as "pioneers on the male frontier." In fields such as steel, construction, and automobiles, women are gaining access to the highest-paying blue-collar jobs. Women in these settings are also entering the craft occupations, traditionally among the highest-paying and most prestigious jobs within the blue-collar sector. For women who enter such jobs, the pressures can be considerable. Traditional male norms may be pervasive, and the problems of being a token can be great. For these reasons, and others that we will discuss later, blue-collar women provide a fascinating case study of current female employment trends.

Our investigation has focused on women in the basic steel industry. Several years ago, following pressure from the federal government, the major steel companies and the steelworker's union agreed to increase the hiring of women, both in entry-level labor jobs and in the craft occupations. For three years, we have studied that situation, focusing on two plants within the industry.

Our first question was whether the change in policy had any effect. In other words, we questioned whether women were being hired in increasing numbers, and whether the women, once hired, were staying on the job. To this end, we conducted numerous interviews with company personnel and collected numerous records of employment, hiring, and terminations.

Beyond these records, we tried to learn more about the day-to-day work in the steel mills. We talked to the workers themselves, both women and men, to learn more about their experiences. In talking to the women, we were interested in how they felt about their jobs, what problems they had experienced, and what rewards they received. From the men, we tried to learn how they felt about the influx of women into their traditionally male domain. And finally, from the supervisors, we attempted to find out what effects the increased number of women have had on productivity and morale, whether any particular problems exist, and what kinds of recruitment and training procedures might be most effective. In the pages that follow, we will describe our findings.

To set the context for "women of steel," we will first look at the work of women more generally. In Chapter 1, we will present a brief history of women's employment in the United States; in Chapter 2, we will consider some of the psychological and social factors that influence women's employment and look at the present involvement of women in white-collar, pink-collar, and blue-collar jobs. To further understand recent trends in female employment, we will review the history of protective legislation and affirmative action in Chapter 3, describing the ways in which public policy has had an impact on the choices that women have and setting the stage for the particular government policies that have been applied to the steel industry. Chapter 4 will provide, for the uninitiated, a brief history of the United States steel industry—an industry that in the past has been synonymous with industrial development and strength but that in recent years has been threatened with shrinking markets and foreign competition.

With Chapter 5, we begin to tell our own story, describing the people whom we studied and the methods that we used. Chapter 6 presents the "big picture"—a statistical analysis of employment trends that considers shifts in the employment of both sexes and of three major ethnic groups. Further in Chapter 6 we will consider the effects of "targeting." Do policies that are intended to benefit one particular group have an adverse effect on another, perhaps previously targeted, group?

Chapters 7, 8, and 9 describe many of the findings of our study of women in the steel mill. In Chapter 7 the focus is on the performance of women in the mills, as viewed by the women themselves, their male coworkers, and their supervisors. In Chapter 8, we look at more subjective indices, in an attempt to learn how women feel about their jobs and what they want for their future. In Chapter 9, we will take a closer look at the craft occupations. Throughout these analyses, we will be comparing our own findings with other discussions of blue-collar workers.

Finally, in Chapter 10 we will consider the implications of our findings. What should policy makers know as they structure legislation that will affect the entry of women into traditionally male blue-collar jobs? And what should managers within those companies consider in their design of hiring policies and training programs? And last, more generally, just what is the future for women in blue-collar jobs?

Through this analysis, we hope to provide an informative account of women holding blue-collar jobs in one particular industry, and more specifically, in two particular plants within that industry. As one particular case, however, our women of steel represent a trend in female employment in the United States. The conditions of their work, their successes and failures, and the perceptions by other people of their contribution are important in understanding the employment of women generally. Further, the particular interface of governmental action and female employment, studied here in one setting, can tell us a great deal about the influence of policy on employment patterns, and serve as a case study for more general understanding of the labor market.

1

A History of Women's Employment in the United States

The dramatic increase in women's labor force participation since World War II and the consequent publicity attending this increase obscure the historical fact that American women have always worked. In the agrarian society that typified America from colonial times to the early 1900s, most women worked in similar ways and often for longer hours than did men. Among farm families, tasks were divided among family members, and all shared in the work of the enterprise from early youth to old age.

With the onset of urbanization and industrialization, much work began to be carried out in larger groups away from the home and farm. Most often men took these jobs, while women stayed home to operate the household. Even though both men and women were obviously working, only paid work has come to be considered true work in our society. As Levitan et al. have noted:

> The low value given to housewives' nonmarket homemaking duties is reflected in the fact that this productive work is not counted in the gross national product or other national accounts, although such services are counted if domestics or others are paid to perform them. If, in 1964, the value of housewives' unpaid services had been counted in monetary terms—by using the wage rates of domestic workers—wives would have added about one-fourth to the GNP. (1981, p. 286)

Women's work as housewives clearly is of enormous economic and social benefit to contemporary American society. At least until very recently, such work surely contributed more in economic terms each year

1

than has the total of women's work outside the home. Nevertheless it is work outside the home that this chapter addresses. It is this work that has increased so dramatically in the past 35 years.

We will survey the history of women's employment in the United States, beginning with the early Colonial period and moving through the growth of the textile industry and the movement of women from home to factory. The changing composition of the work force and the continuous redefinition of appropriate women's work will be traced through the nineteenth and twentieth century. Of particular interest will be the World War II period that put "Rosie the Riveter" in the forefront. Finally, we will survey the period from World War II to the present, looking in more detail at the current patterns of employment for women.[1]

WOMEN'S WORK PRIOR TO 1900

Despite the predominance of women working on family farms or as urban homemakers, American women have a long record of work outside the home. In fact, as writers from Abbott (1910) to Kessler-Harris (1981) have noted, some women have always worked outside the family enterprise. Nor has such work always been in occupations related to women's domestic roles, such as teachers, nurses, or cooks. Rather, as Edith Abbott pointed out in her classic volume on women in industry, "Under every industrial system, women have had a recognized position" (1910, p. 2).

The women who immigrated to the United States in the sixteenth and seventeenth centuries were not a leisure class. These women, whether white women accompanying their husbands to begin a new life with more economic opportunity and less religious persecution, or black women who were first brought to the New World as slaves in 1619, immediately went to work (Wertheimer, 1977). Although most of this work was domestic or agricultural, some women were gainfully employed away from the home or farm. Wertheimer (1977) describes women who ran inns, operated printing presses, ground eyeglasses, and worked as undertakers.

The equal involvement of men and women in work was in part a necessity, emerging from the need to carve out a livelihood in a sometimes-hostile and previously unsettled environment. Beyond this necessity, the spirit of Puritanism that drove many people to the New World decried idleness and demanded that all able-bodied people work, a mandate often backed up with official laws and edicts (Wertheimer, 1977). As Kessler-Harris observes, "The Puritans acknowledged women as partners in a joint enterprise and recognized domestic works as essential to survival" (1982, p. 7).

For other women, primarily black women, it was not religious wrath or

Puritan spirit that put them to work, but rather servitude, as thousands of African women and men were brought to America as indentured servants or slaves to swell the colonial labor force. In a somewhat unusual reversal, the women were valued more than the men and commanded higher prices at slave auctions (Kessler-Harris, 1982). Their value was, of course, tied to the slavery system: if a plantation owner could keep a slave for life, then in buying a female slave he would buy "reproductive rights" as well, thus eventually gaining several slaves for the price of one woman.

In the late eighteenth and early nineteenth century, the pattern of employment for women began to change, at least for white women in the North. Sewing and weaving that had first been primarily for family consumption expanded, and women began to produce more than they needed. The surplus was sold to merchants who collected work from many women and sold it from a central location, collecting at the same time a profit for themselves. Before long, factories opened that could centralize the production of the material as well, and to staff these factories, women and children were sought. The Protestant ethic continued to exert its influence in encouraging this movement into the factory. This ethic was evident in the comments of Alexander Hamilton in 1791: "It is worthy of particular remark that in general women and children are rendered more useful, and the latter more easily useful, by manufacturing establishments than they would otherwise be" (Wertheimer, 1977, p. 50). Somewhat more blatantly, advertisements for the first cotton factory in Beverly, Massachusetts suggested that it would "afford employment to a great number of women and children, many of whom will be otherwise unless, if not burdensome to society" (Abbott, 1910, p. 43).

Technology allowed and encouraged the development of the factory system. In 1793, the cotton gin was invented; in 1814, the first power loom was installed in Waltham, Massachusetts. Thus the textile industry began its growth with labor supplied primarily by women and children. As Abbott noted:

> The result of the introduction of the factory system in the textile industries was that the work which women had been doing in the home could be done more efficiently outside of the home, but women were carrying on the same processes in the making of yarn or cloth. (1910, p. 47)

The Protestant ethic decreed the work ethic for everyone, and production of textiles was indeed a continuation of the work that women had been doing in the home. At the same time, it is important to consider why men were not attracted to the mills in the same numbers as women. In part, this may have been due to the sex-linked nature of the work. In addition, however, men had other options, among them the vocation of farming, highly valued during this period in both social and economic terms. "Female aid in manufactures," one observer noted, "prevents the diversion of men and boys from agriculture" (quoted in Kessler-Harris, 1982, p. 24).

The women of Lowell, Massachusetts epitomized the new trend in female employment (Dublin, 1979; Kessler-Harris, 1981, 1982). Appealing to young, single women, Francis Cabot Lowell opened his mill in 1821, together with a boardinghouse system in which these women could stay under appropriate moral supervision. It was not anticipated that these women would become a permanent part of the paid labor force; rather it was assumed that they would work for a few years, send money back to their families, or save for a dowry, and then return to their farm to get married and maintain a home. The wages at the time were considered reasonably good, although as the factory system expanded, the work demands increased and boarding rates were raised without a corresponding increase in salary levels.

Generally speaking, the first half of the nineteenth century was a period in which, to use Abbott's (1910) term, the factory system was "domesticated." Machinery was applied to many different industries, and often women were brought in to operate these machines. In the period from 1820 to 1840, more than 100 industrial occupations were open to women, most of them dealing with the manufacture of small objects such as straw hats, buttons, and braid (Abbott, 1910). In the textile industry, where women first worked in factories, they outnumbered men by two to one by 1831; by 1850 50 percent of all manufacturing workers were women (Baxandall, Gordon, and Reverby, 1976). To put these numbers in perspective, it should be pointed out that a rough estimate for 1830 showed white women's labor force participation rate at 10 percent. Virtually all black women, being slaves, were workers. By 1870, the participation rate for all women 16 years and over was 15 percent (Lebergott, 1964).

Around mid-century some changes in the female employment pattern occurred. The "Lowell" model became increasingly unattractive for women from farm and middle-class families, as wages were reduced and working conditions deteriorated. In Lowell, 800 women left in 1834 and 1500 more in 1836, protesting an increase in board with no concomitant increase in wages (Kessler-Harris, 1982). It has also been argued that new conceptions of women and family began to develop during this period, at least among the middle- and upper-class (Kessler-Harris, 1981, 1982). As more men moved into the industrial sector, the importance of the roles of mother and wife were stressed, and the primary duty of the woman was seen to be the rearing of children. At the same time, "ladyhood" was fostered, shifting the role of wife from an equal helpmate to someone more subject to the wishes and will of the husband. The household was now transformed, Kessler-

Harris writes, "from a place where productive labor was performed to one whose main goals were the preservation of virtue and morality (1981, p. 39).

With middle-class women no longer as willing to go into the factories, new sources of labor had to be sought. Immigration solved the problem for factory owners. Between 1840 and 1860, over four million immigrants entered the United States, 40 percent of whom were Irish fleeing from the potato famines (Kessler-Harris, 1982). By the 1850s, much of the "factory work was done by immigrant women and was considered off limits for native-born Americans" (Kessler-Harris, 1981, p. 61). In Lowell, for example, more than half of the work force was foreign-born by 1852. Black women joined the working ranks of the foreign-born during the latter part of the century, as many black families moved north and west to cities after the Civil War.

As would be true of later wars, the Civil War opened up some new job opportunities for women. As Elizabeth Massey observed at that time, "The war did more in four years to change [women's] economic status than had been accomplished in any preceding generation" (quoted in Kessler-Harris, 1982, p. 76). Many of these new jobs were in professional and semi-professional fields. The federal government allowed women to enter clerical jobs; nursing became a recognized profession, and the number of female teachers increased sharply.

By 1900, 20 percent of American women 14 years and older were employed outside the home, and they constituted 18 percent of the total labor force (Oppenheimer, 1970). Nearly 50 percent of these women were first- or second-generation immigrants, 15 percent were black, and approximately one-third were native-born whites (Kessler-Harris, 1981). Given that approximately 55 percent of the female population in 1900 was native-born, it is clear that there were marked differences in the conditions under which women worked. The cults of motherhood and ladyhood seem indeed to have made inroads among middle- and upper-class white women. Federal investigations in 1910–14 concluded that the majority of wage-earning women were poor and single (Kessler-Harris, 1982).

Many of the working women were in manufacturing, particularly in the textile factories of the North and the tobacco factories of the South. Women also worked in other industries, such as shoes, canning, and even in the iron and steel industry. At the same time, it should be noted that the most likely occupation for a woman at that time was servant, accounting for more than 28 percent of the female labor force (Oppenheimer, 1970; Baxandall et al., 1976). The next four most "popular" occupations for women in 1900 were farm laborer (as a family member), dressmaker, teacher, and laundry worker. Thus, even though women made early inroads into manufacturing jobs, they were already concentrated in a limited number of sex-segregated jobs. In 1900, for example, all dressmakers and milliners were women; 94 percent of nurses were women; 97 percent of private household workers were women; and 80 percent of telephone operators were women. Even in secretarial work, which had been a predominantly male occupation until the Civil War, women now accounted for 72 percent of the job holders (Oppenheimer, 1970). Most of these jobs would continue to be sex-segregated 50 years later.

FROM 1900 TO WORLD WAR II

Between 1900 and 1940, the labor force participation of women grew slowly but steadily, and by 1940, approximately 25 percent of women were in the labor force. Nearly half of these women were single; another third were either widowed, divorced, or had husbands absent for some other reason, a pattern not terribly different from that of 1900 (Oppenheimer, 1970).

The occupations in which women were concentrated changed somewhat during this period, reflecting growth in various sectors of the economy. Although servant continued to be the number one occupation for women in 1940, typist and secretary, and other types of clerical workers, as well as bookkeeper, accountant, and cashier were among the leading occupations. Other common employment positions for women were teacher, sales personnel, and waitress, the latter appearing for the first time in 1940 as one of the top ten occupations for women (Baxandall et al., 1976).

The job of semiskilled machine operator and others like it in the apparel and accessory industries were also among the leaders, continuing a trend that had begun in Lowell and other New England towns. The importance of this field for women was also evidenced in the growth of trade unions for women during this period, shown most clearly in the founding of the International Ladies' Garment Workers Union. Although the union was originally founded in 1900, it came to prominence a decade later, during the historic strike of the New York shirtwaist workers in the winter of 1909–10 (Wertheimer, 1977).

This strike, protesting working conditions in the New York garment industry, was later referred to as the "uprising of the 20,000" and proved to be a catalyst for union organization. Further impetus came in the wake of a tragic fire at the Triangle Shirtwaist Company in New York, in which 146 people—mostly women and young girls—were killed. By 1913, the International Ladies' Garment Workers Union claimed 90,000 members (not all of whom were women). During the first 20 years of this century, the union movement became increasingly active. In many cases, however, women were not central to the movement, in part because they still did not have the vote and hence were not considered full citizens, and in part because they were often considered only temporary members of the work force (Baxandall et al., 1976).

War—this time World War I—again was a stimulant for female employment. Again, jobs that had previously been closed to women were opened up, if only temporarily. The range of these new opportunities was broad, from banking and finance to durable manufacturing. As the Women's Bureau noted in 1920, the war had "forced the experiment of woman labor in the craftsmanly occupations" (quoted in Kessler-Harris, 1982, p. 219). Thus, while the numbers of working women did not increase dramatically during this period, the types of occupations did show some marked shifts. At the end of the war, however, most of these traditionally male jobs became dominated by males once again. As molders in one iron factory argued to their employers, "You would not let your daughter or wife go into it, neither would I, neither would any other of these people" (quoted in Kessler-Harris, 1982, p. 232). Although factory jobs were not a possibility for most women, the postwar economic growth did create a large number of jobs in areas that were open to women, primarily in white-collar office work (Kessler-Harris, 1982).

Most women who were married still did not work. In 1920, only 9 percent of married women with husbands present in the home were reported to be in the labor force (Kessler-Harris, 1981). When the depression hit, these married women were particularly vulnerable. Popular opinion held that it was unfair for two people in a single family to be earning wages when many families had no income at all. Norman Cousins presented this logic quite clearly:

> There are approximately 10,000,000 people out of work in the United States today; there are also 10,000,000 or more women, married and single, who are jobholders. Simply fire the women, who shouldn't be working anyway, and hire the men. Presto! No unemployment. No relief rolls. No depression.
>
> (Quoted in Kessler-Harris, 1982, p. 256)

Legislators in 26 states introduced bills against married women workers, although only one of these passed and that one was later repealed (Baxandall et al., 1976). More effectively, a 1932 federal executive order ruled that only one spouse could work for the government, and many women did in fact lose their jobs (Kessler-Harris, 1981). Many other formal and informal policies by individual employers led to either the refusal to hire married women or the dismissal of women who were married or who chose to get married during this period. Thus "in the early years of the depression, women lost their jobs and stayed unemployed at almost double the rate of men" (Kessler-Harris, 1981, p. 139). Yet despite these temporary setbacks, the proportion of women in the labor force resumed its steady growth as World War II approached.

THE EVENTS OF WORLD WAR II

If the Depression era was the worst of times for women workers, then World War II was in many ways the best of times. As men were drafted, enlisted, and removed from the resident labor force, industry demanded an influx of new workers, and women responded to the demand. Although employers in heavy industry were at first reluctant to hire women to fill jobs that had traditionally been the domain of men, necessity led to innovation.

Both government propaganda and the media fostered this transition (Rupp, 1978). A billboard of that era displayed the following message:

What Job is mine on the Victory line?
If you've sewed on buttons, or made buttonholes, on a machine, you can learn to do spot welding on airplane parts.
If you've used an electric mixer in your kitchen, you can learn to run a drill press.
If you've followed recipes exactly in making cakes, you can learn to load shell.

(Baxandall et al., 1976, p. 284)

Fortune magazine proclaimed that "the margin now is woman power" (Kessler-Harris, 1981, p. 141). National public opinion polls showed that 60 percent of the population approved of married women working in the war industry (Oppenheimer, 1970). For women, it became a patriotic duty to enter the working world.

Women responded to these appeals, not only for reasons of patriotism, but for financial reasons as well. Nearly five million female workers entered the labor force for the first time during this period (Kessler-Harris, 1982). For many other women, available jobs in industry, construction, and shipbuilding meant the opportunity to move from lower-paying jobs as domestics, launderers, and garment workers to jobs in the factories that would pay as much as 40 percent more than their traditional jobs. In heavy industry, the number of women working grew from 340,000 to over two million in just a few years (Baker, 1978). By 1945, 38 percent of all women over 16 years of age were in the labor force, constituting 36 percent of all workers (Blau, 1978). Nearly 20 million women were wage earners, a peak that would not be reached again for nearly a decade. Thus was Rosie the Riveter born in the imagination of the American public.

The demographic characteristics of working women changed dramatically during this period as well. Black women, previously relegated to a limited number of jobs, were able to enter the manufacturing sector for the first time. Whereas before the war, 72 percent of employed black women were household workers, only 48 percent were so employed at the end of the war (Baker, 1978). Such moves were not made without prejudice and discrimination. In some cases, separate plants were established for blacks and whites. In other cases, specific quotas were set for the employment of black workers. Yet despite these barriers, black women did gain access to the industrial sector.

Married women also entered the labor force in unprecedented numbers. Whereas single women had constituted the bulk of working women throughout the nineteenth and early twentieth century, the war effort made work both respectable and necessary for married women as well. More than three million married women entered the labor force between 1940 and 1944 (Baxandall et al., 1976). Some structural changes were made, if only temporarily, to encourage married women to work. Many industrial plants established day-care centers, where women could leave their children while they worked. Although many of these centers were inadequate and most were temporary, they did allow some women to combine the roles of worker and mother in a way that might not otherwise have been possible. Federal funding was also supplied to support child-care facilities; it is estimated that more than a half a million children were served by federally supported programs during the wartime period (Baxandall et al., 1976).

Other segments of the economy also were responsive to the work situation of married women. Thus, "to correct conditions such as Mrs. War Worker often faces, local industries are cooperating in many places to provide night shopping hours for industrial workers" (Blood, in Baxandall et al., 1976, p. 295). Other perquisites sometimes available to the woman worker included grocery stores, beauty shops, and shoe-repair facilities established at plant locations, and the dispatch of representatives from grocery stores to the plants where orders could be taken for later delivery.

The end of the war marked the end of the zealous support for the woman worker. As diplomatic peace treaties were signed, hundreds of thousands of men returned to the States, anticipating a return to their prewar jobs. Although some women willingly left their jobs and returned to the home, many others were not eager to relinquish their wartime jobs. In 1944–45 the Women's Bureau of the federal goverment conducted an intensive study of the women who were working. The results of this study showed that about 75 percent of the women expected to continue to work. Furthermore, the majority of these women wanted to continue to work in the same areas in which they had been working, rather than return to the jobs that they had held before the war. As the report of the Women's Bureau noted, "Postwar job openings as cafeteria bus girls . . . are not apt to prove attractive to women who are seeking work as screw-machine operators" (Baxandall et al., 1976, p. 311). This expectation of continued employment was particularly strong among some groups of women. Black women, for example, were more likely than white women to plan continued work. Nearly all single, widowed, and divorced women planned to continue work. Further, 11 percent of the married women were the sole wage earner in their family, and these women also wanted to continue in the work force. The reasons for these plans are clear. For many women, particularly those in the groups just noted, responsibility for support of themselves and others was a primary reason for work plans. Work, in other words, was a necessity.

The hopes of these women to maintain their wartime jobs did not materialize, however. Men were rehired in their former jobs, and many women were forced to return to lower-paying, traditionally female jobs. Although women in unionized industries filed hundreds of grievances, seniority rules gave preference to returning veterans and the women were generally let go. Government supports that existed during the war, such as the federal funding of day-care programs, were withdrawn. During the war years, over three thousand day-care centers were operating; 2,800 of these were closed after the war ended (Baker, 1978). Media that had hailed Rosie the Riveter only a few years before now proclaimed the value of home and family (Rupp, 1978). Magazines such as *Good Housekeeping* ran stories on "Why I Quit Working," in which the author noted the benefits of the role of wife and mother: the "normalcy" of relationships, the luxury of free time and leisure, and improved appearance. "Slowly," wrote one such author, "I'm learning to forget the meaning of the word tension. While I was working, I was tense from the moment I woke up in the morning until I fell into bed at night (Colton, in Baxandall et al., 1976, p. 302).

Statistics show the drop in female employment. From a wartime high of 38 percent labor force participation, the percentage of women workers dropped to 31 percent by 1947. Not until 1953 did the number of women workers exceed that of the wartime period (Blau, 1978). The occupational profile of women workers changed as well. In most cases, the percentage of women in heavy industry fell back to its prewar level.[2] Thus in 1950, the primary occupations of women were similar to those of earlier years with typist, clerical worker, sales clerk, private household worker, elementary teacher, and waitress leading the list.

THE PAST THREE DECADES

Although the percentage of women in the work force dropped in the years immediately following World War II, the decrease was only temporary. From 1950 to the present, there has been a steady increase in the percentage of women in the labor force. As Table 1.1 shows, 51.7 percent of all women over 16 years of age were in the labor force in 1980.

The pattern of women's labor force participation has changed almost as dramatically as the proportion of participation. In 1947, female labor force participation peaked at age 18 or 19 at just over 50 percent, and then declined rapidly to a low of about 30 percent in the late 1920s and early 1930s. This behavior closely paralleled the ages of marriage and child-bearing. From age 35 to 44, women's labor force participation in this era rose to about 35 percent as women returned to the labor force when their children matured (U.S. Department of Labor, 1979).

In the past three decades, the peak labor force participation has not only become much higher than in 1947 (about 69 percent versus 50 percent), but high participation rates have continued without the marked drop formerly associated with marriage and childbearing ages. Peak participation in 1980 was among 20–24 year olds. The rising participation rate in this age group reflects delayed marriages, deferral of first births, and smaller family sizes.

Between the ages of 25 and 54, labor force participation by women is now quite stable, both in comparison with former times and in an absolute sense. This is the same pattern of participation long exhibited by men, a pattern of sustained labor force participation subsequent to a period of education and training in the teens and early twenties. In recent years, the sharpest increase in participation has come among married women with young children. Between 1960 and 1975, the percentage of working married women with children under the age of six more than doubled. By 1975, 33 percent of women with children under three were working, as were 42 percent of women with children between the ages of three and five (Almquist, 1977).

Further evidence of the increased career orientation of women may be seen in school enrollment data. In 1950, only 8 percent of the 20–24-year-old women not in the labor force were enrolled in school. In 1980, 38 percent of women in this same age group who were not in the labor force gave being enrolled in school as the reason for their not working. Thus, among young women not actually in the labor force, preparation for work in the form of schooling is an increasingly prominent reason for their lack of participation. In 1950, 52 percent of women in the 20–24 age group were either in the labor force or in school or both, compared to 77 percent in 1980 (U.S. Department of Labor, January 1981).

TABLE 1.1 Female Labor Force Participation Rates, by Age, 1900–80

	1900 (%)	1940 (%)	1950 (%)	1960 (%)	1970 (%)	1980 (%)
Total, 14 years and older (16 and older from 1970)	20.0	25.8	29.0	34.5	43.4	51.7
14–24 years (16–24 from 1970)	29.0	30.8	32.5	32.5	51.4	62.2
25–34 years	19.4	33.3	31.8	35.3	45.0	65.5
35–44 years	15.0	27.2	35.0	42.6	51.1	65.5
45–54 years	14.2	22.5	32.9	46.6	54.4	59.9
55–64 years	12.6	16.8	23.4	35.0	43.0	41.5
65 years and over	8.3	6.1	7.8	10.3	9.7	8.1

Sources: Oppenheimer, 1970, for 1900–1960; U.S. Department of Labor, 1971; U.S. Department of Labor, April 1981, for 1980.

Many factors have led to the rise in female labor force participation since World War II. Some writers (e.g., Oppenheimer, 1970) stress the importance of changes on the demand side, for example, the structure, location, and requirements of jobs. Demand in traditional female occupations such as clerical work, teaching, and nursing have grown much faster than demand for workers in general. As an example, clerical jobs constituted 12 percent of all employment in 1947, compared with 18 percent in 1980. Similarly, the fastest-growing industries in recent decades have been those that have historically hired a high percentage of women. Employment in service industries grew by over 21 million workers from 1957 to 1980, whereas manufacturing, mining, and construction employment combined grew by only 7 million in the same period. Women accounted for only 26 percent of employment in manufacturing, mining, and construction in 1980, compared with a 61 percent share of service industry employment (U.S. Department of Labor, January 1981).

Social and cultural factors have also contributed to the sharp rise in women's labor force participation since World War II. As noted earlier, women participated in a broad spectrum of jobs during that war, and participated at a higher rate than they previously had. The exploits of "Rosie the Riveter" and her peers legitimized women working to some extent, despite the media-backed efforts to return to the status quo. Changing patterns of legislation also allowed women to pursue more employment opportunities (see Chapter 3).

The marked increase in female-headed families, and the older ages at which women first marry, are also important factors affecting women's labor force participation. One-fourth of the female labor force is currently single and 20 percent are divorced, separated, or widowed. At present, 8.5 million women are family heads, accounting for one of every seven families. For most of these women, labor force participation is a necessity, quite aside from their individual preferences.

Many married women have entered the labor market for economic reasons as well, seeking to maintain family real income that has been eroded by inflation. Finally, many women have stronger aspirations to work outside the home for reasons other than necessity. The rising educational level of the female population provides both skills needed in the work force and higher levels of motivation.

OCCUPATIONAL AND INCOME DISTRIBUTION OF WOMEN'S EMPLOYMENT

Despite the great increase in women's labor force activity, the distribution of women's occupations has remained quite stable. Nor have women ignored their earnings relative to men as they have increased their participation in the labor market. As Table 1.2 indicates, men and women are distributed differently across the broad occupational spectrum. This difference is an important factor accounting for the gap in earnings between women and men, as well as an indicator of the impact of discrimination (Levitan, Mangum & Marshall, 1981). In 1980, over half of all women were in clerical or service jobs; in contrast, these occupational groups employed only 15 percent of male workers. The extent of occupational concentration of women can be seen in Table 1.3, which shows the ten occupations with the highest concentration of women in 1970 (Baxandall et al., 1976). In total, these ten occupations contained over 35 percent of all employed women in 1980. The predominance of women in certain occupations is remarkably persistent over time. Oppenheimer (1970) found that occupations that were primarily held by women in 1900 (for example, dressmaker, private household worker, nurse, telephone operator, secretary, typist, teacher, and librarian) were still exclusive female domains a half century later.

It is also important to note that even among women, there are different occupational distributions as a function of ethnic group, as shown in Table 1.4. Black and other minority women are far more likely to be service workers and less likely to hold white-collar jobs. However, these differences have been decreasing. From 1964 to 1980, for example, the percentage of black and minority women holding service jobs fell from 56 percent to 31 percent, while the percentage holding clerical jobs increased from 11 percent to 29 percent. During this same period, the occupational pattern of

TABLE 1.2   Occupations of Employed Males and Females, 1980 (in percentages)

	Females	Males
White-collar workers	65.6	42.4
Professional/technical	16.8	15.5
Managers/administrators	6.9	14.4
Sales workers	6.8	6.0
Clerical workers	35.1	6.4
Blue-collar workers	13.8	44.8
Craft workers	1.8	21.0
Operatives (except transport)	10.0	11.1
Transport equipment operatives	.7	5.7
Laborers	1.2	7.0
Service workers	19.5	8.8
Farm workers	1.2	4.0

Source: U.S. Department of Labor, January 1981.

TABLE 1.3 Occupations that Employed Largest Number of Women in 1970

Occupation	Number Employed 1980	Percent Women 1980
Secretaries	3,876,000	99.1
Retail sales clerks	2,343,000	71.1
Bookkeepers	1,906,000	90.5
Cashiers	1,554,000	86.6
Waiters	1,416,000	89.1
Elementary school teachers	1,383,000	83.7
Registered nurses	1,302,000	96.5
Private household workers	1,041,000	97.5
Typists	1,023,000	96.9
Sewers and stitchers	788,000	95.7

Source: U.S. Department of Labor, April 1981.

TABLE 1.4 Occupations of Employed White and Minority Women, 1980 (in percentages)

	White	Black and Other Minority
White-collar workers	67.7	50.9
Professional/technical	17.0	14.8
Managers/administrators	7.4	3.7
Sales workers	7.3	3.1
Clerical workers	36.0	29.3
Blue-collar workers	13.2	17.7
Craft workers	1.9	1.4
Operatives (except transport)	9.4	14.3
Transport equipment operatives	.7	.6
Laborers	1.2	1.4
Service workers	17.8	30.8
Farm workers	1.3	.6
Total numbers	36,043,000	5,239,000

Source: U.S. Department of Labor, January 1981.

white women stayed relatively constant, indicating more significant changes in the qualitative employment picture for black and minority women during the past two decades. At present, ethnicity appears to be a less important predictor for women than men.

The distribution of women in broad occupational groups has changed somewhat since 1940, as Table 1.5 indicates. Several observations can be made. First, even though women can now be found in virtually every occupation, most of the growth has been concentrated in traditionally female occupations. Oppenheimer (1970) estimates that almost half of the net increase in employed women between 1950 and 1960 occurred in occupations in which at least 70 percent of the workers were women. Second, it can be seen that women have been conspicuously unsuccessful in acquiring a substantially larger share of the skilled craft jobs. As will be discussed at greater length in Chapter 9, women craft workers are concentrated in a few specific trades. In many crafts, women have no more than 1 percent of the jobs. Finally, women's share of professional and

TABLE 1.5   Distribution of Employed Women by Occupation 1940 and 1980

Major Occupational Group	Percent of Women Employed in Occupational Group		Women as a Percent of Total Workers in Occupational Group	
	1980	*1940*	*1980*	*1940*
Total Number (in thousands)	41,283	11,920	—	—
Percent	100.0	100.0	42.4	25.9
White-collar workers				
Professional/technical	16.8	13.2	44.3	45.4
Managers and administrators	6.9	3.8	26.1	11.7
Clerical	35.1	21.2	80.1	52.6
Sales	6.8	7.0	45.3	27.9
Blue-collar workers				
Craft workers	1.8	0.9	6.0	2.1
Operatives	10.7	18.4	30.4	25.7
Nonfarm laborers	1.2	0.8	11.6	3.2
Service workers				
Private household	2.5	17.6	97.4	93.8
Other	17.0	11.3	58.9	40.1
Farm workers	1.2	5.8	18.0	8.0

Sources: Bureau of Labor Statistics, 1975b; U.S. Department of Labor, April 1981.

technical jobs has actually declined slightly since 1940 (although the absolute numbers have obviously increased). Most professional women workers are still concentrated in the fields of health and elementary education.

One consequence of the disparate occupational distribution of women and men is that women earn much less than men on the average. Indeed, for several decades, women working on a full-time, full-year basis have earned approximately 60 percent of what men have earned. The historical antecedents of this modern ratio are striking. In the Bible, Leviticus describes an assessment of the worth of males and females by the Lord and Moses, in which a male is valued at fifty shekels of silver and a female at thirty shekels (Barrett, 1979). Similarly, records of nineteenth-century England show that women's wages were set at 60 percent of men's, presumably because women's needs were less (Barrett, 1979).

Distressingly, women's income as a proportion of men's has actually fallen in recent decades. In 1956 women earned 63 percent as much as men, whereas in 1978 they earned only 59 percent as much. Further, a breakdown of salaries by occupational groups reveals that women's earnings relative to men's have declined in almost every occupational category.

A recent Bureau of Labor Statistics press release (1982) shows the extent to which women earn less than men at both broad and detailed occupational levels. The report is based on an analysis of usual weekly earnings as reported in the Current Population Survey, a monthly survey of households conducted by the U.S. Census Bureau. The earnings are for wage and salary workers employed full time (i.e., 35 or more hours per week), and exclude self-employed workers. These comparative earnings are shown in Table 1.6.

Women earn less than men in each of the more than 100 occupations listed in the Labor Department report. Similarly, the upper end of the scale is different for women and men. The average weekly wage earned by male aerospace and aeronautical engineers, the highest-paid occupation for men, is $619. The highest-paid occupation for women, operations and systems researchers and analysts, paid female incumbents $422 per week.

Despite its historical precedence, the continuing and pervasive disparity between the wages of women and men is of considerable concern. One consequence is that many women are living in poverty or near-poverty conditions, often while supporting children without the help of a spouse. In 1977, for example, 53 percent of full-time year-round women workers were earning less than $10,000; the corresponding figure for men was 19 percent (Barrett, 1979). At the other end of the distribution, only 10 percent of women were making more than $15,000, while 48 percent of men fell in this category (Barrett, 1979). Furthermore, the wages of women change little over the course of their working careers. As Figure 1.1 indicates, the earning pattern of women is relatively flat. For men, in contrast, average earnings continue to rise as they approach mid-life, falling only after they reach approximately 50 years of age.

TABLE 1.6a   Median Weekly Earnings Reported for Men and Women for 1981 for Major Occupational Groups

	Men	Women	Women's Earnings as Percent of Men's Earnings
Professional and technical workers	$439	$316	71.8%
Managers and administrators	466	283	60.8
Craft workers	360	239	66.5
Machine operatives	298	187	62.9
Nonfarm laborers	244	193	79.3
Service workers except private household	238	170	71.3
Farm workers	180	146	81.1

TABLE 1.6b   Median Earnings in a Sample of Detailed Occupations[a]

	Men	Women	Women percent of men's earnings
Accountants	433	308	71.2%
Computer specialists	488	355	72.8
Engineers	547	371	67.8
College teachers	384	311	80.9
Restaurant & bar managers	312	223	71.6
Statistical clerks	326	227	69.7
Cashiers	180	166	92.0
Assemblers	297	205	69.0
Textile workers	229	186	81.3
Material handlers	266	207	78.0
Nursing aids & attendants	203	167	82.2

[a]Women's earnings included only for occupations employing 50,000 women or more.
Source: Bureau of Labor Statistics, 1982.

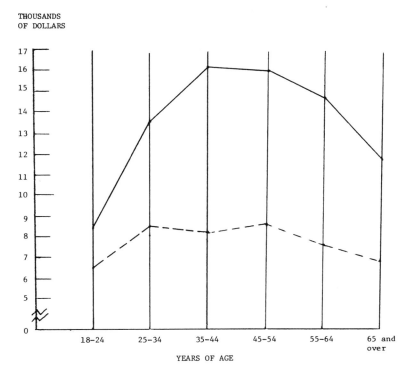

FIGURE 1.1   Life-Cycle Earnings Profiles of Men and Women, 1975
(Mean Earnings of Full-Time, Year-Round Men and Women by Age)

Source: Reprinted from R. E. Smith (ed.), *The subtle revolution: Women at work*, The Urban Institute (1979), p. 37.

THE FUTURE OF WORKING WOMEN

All projections indicate that the increase in the proportion of women in the labor force will continue (Smith, 1979). By 1995, it is predicted that 61 percent of women will be in the labor force, accounting for nearly 60 million women (Fullerton, 1980). What does the future hold for these women? Will they continue to be concentrated in the same occupations that they are today? Will women continue to earn substantially less than men, even when working in the same occupation as men?

Such questions cannot be answered with certainty. The continued growth of service industries, for example, would suggest that women may continue to be concentrated in these typically low-wage jobs. At the same time, other forces are at work that may foreshadow greater diversification and higher wages. The increasing educational levels of women, particularly the rapid growth of enrollment in graduate professional schools, suggests a subsequent surge in employment of women in highly paid professional jobs. According to a recent article in *Business Week*, the percentage of advanced accounting degrees awarded to women grew from 7 percent in 1969 to 28 percent in 1980. In business, the number of graduate degrees received by women rose from 3 percent to 23 percent in the same period. In medicine, the comparable figures were 8 percent and 24 percent. It seems highly likely that these figures will translate into income gains for women both on the average and compared to their male counterparts in these occupations.

The attitudes of people toward women working have shown some change in a positive direction over the past several years, and although these changes appear to be levelling off, the past increase in liberality may influence future generations of women workers. Finally, the enforcement of equal opportunity laws, if consistently applied, could increase the number of women in high-wage fields that have formerly been male domains. The success or failure of the women pioneers who are now entering the traditional male occupations—one group of whom are the subjects of the latter half of this book—may well provide a key to the future of women in the labor force through the end of the twentieth century.

NOTES

1. In a single chapter, we can present only a brief overview of the history of women's employment to set the context for present blue-collar workers in heavy industry. A number of excellent in-depth treatments of this area are available, several of which are cited in this chapter.

2. In some heavy industries, women who had entered clerical jobs for the first time during World War II were able to keep these jobs after the war. An official of one of the steel companies participating in the present study noted that female clerical employment in that firm dated from the World War II era. Prior to that time, virtually all workers including clerical workers had been men.

2

Working Women:
Psychological and
Social Factors

The history of women and work provides an overview of female employment: what jobs women have held, how occupational specialization has developed, and how historical events and social trends have altered the patterns of female employment. It does not, however, provide a very clear sense of the feelings that women have about their employment and the particular problems and conflicts that they may face. For that information, we turn to more recent psychological and sociological literature—to studies that have asked women why they work, why they choose the jobs they do, and what kinds of problems they encounter in their work.

In this chapter we will first consider some of the issues that are common to most working women, such as job and career choice, job satisfaction, and job environment. Then we will look more carefully at some features that are specific to certain groups of working women: first, to the white-collar worker, then the pink-collar worker, and finally the blue-collar worker. This material will provide a frame of reference for later consideration of one particular group of blue-collar women, the women of steel.

ISSUES FOR WAGE-EARNING WOMEN

Although researchers have traditionally devoted less attention to working women than to working men, the continued growth of women in the labor force has resulted in an increase in scientific investigation. Many of the issues that concern wage-earning women, of course, concern wage-earning men as well. Thus issues of career choice and job satisfaction are important issues for everyone in the work force. Yet because of the specific conditions of women's employment—for example, occupational segregation and job discrimination—these questions can take on special meaning in the context of working women. Other issues are more particular to the situation of women. A great deal of attention has been given, for example, to the pressures involved in combining work and family roles. Although this is an issue that logically might be considered relevant to men as well, it is one that is rarely discussed in the context of male employment. For women, it has been a dominant theme, reflecting long-standing beliefs and norms about women's role in the home. Another issue of particular relevance to women is sexual harassment. Recognition of this problem has increased in recent years, and there is now more information about the incidence and consequences of such interactions for the employed woman.

Decisions to Work and Career Choice

The decision to work is, for women as for men, often based on economic necessity. Certainly for women who are single, divorced, widowed, or who for other reasons have no means of support, the decision to work is nearly as automatic as it is for men. Even for women who are married, money is often cited as the primary reason for employment (Nieva & Gutek, 1981). Indeed, it is frequently only with two incomes that the family rises above the poverty level.

Demographic studies have pointed to a number of factors that tend to be characteristic of the women who work. In the past, as was discussed in Chapter 1, women who were young and unmarried were more likely to work than were older married women. Yet that difference has decreased substantially in recent years. Of the women in the labor force in 1979, 55 percent were currently married. Other demographic factors that bear some relationship to working status among women include level of education and mother's employment. Women who have completed college are very likely to be in the labor market: in 1979, approximately two-thirds of women with four or more years of college were in the labor force. In general, college-educated women have greater earning potential than less educated women, providing one reason for this difference (Crowley, 1982). Education is particularly likely to be predictive of labor force participation among married women. Kreps and Clark (1975) report that the labor force participation rate of married women in 1972 increased in accordance with women's education, from 32 percent for women with less than four years of high school to 45 percent for women with high school diplomas, up to 55 percent for women with four or more years of college. Other studies have shown that women are more likely to work if their mothers also worked. Such a pattern may either reflect a modeling effect, whereby the mother provides an example for the daughter, or may simply indicate a common socioeconomic background, whereby work is more necessary for some groups than others.

Ethnic background is also predictive of labor force participation. As early as 1910, 55 percent of black women were in the civilian labor force, compared to only 20 percent of white women (Douglas, 1980). In 1979, the figure for black women was 53 percent. Thus the recent rise in female employment, described in the previous chapter, is primarily attributable to changes in the participation of white women. Black women also spend more years in the labor force on the average, and their participation is less influenced by marital status (Douglas, 1980). In contrast, the labor force participation rate of Hispanic women (specifically those of Mexican or Puerto Rican origin) tends to be lower than that of either white or black women (Almquist & Wehrle-Einhorn, 1978).

For any women, a decision to work can only be realized in the context of job availability. Thus in order for women to work, there must be available jobs and there must be the willingness of employers to hire women (Nieva & Gutek, 1981). Traditionally, the jobs available to women have been fairly limited. The affirmative action activities of the 1970s (see Chapter 3) have in large part been directed at those segments of the labor market that were traditionally closed to women, either by official policy or by custom.

Such limitations in the market undoubtedly have a great deal to do with the process of career choice for women. Unfortunately, studies of job or career choice have very often been limited to college students, and thus relatively little is known about the aspirations of women (or men) for jobs in which college is not required preparation. However, even studies with younger children have shown a narrower range of career thoughts for girls than for boys (Nieva & Gutek, 1981). Furthermore, educational programs at the primary and secondary level and vocational counseling may present different options, posing specific patterns according to sex and race (Baker, 1978; Douglas, 1980; Gurin, 1981).

Past studies of career choice among women have generally been unsatisfactory. In part, this condition is based on insufficient attention to women's careers. It has also been the case, however, that studies have often found less regularity in the work pattern of women. As a result of these discontinuities, many investigators have chosen to focus on the women who are "pioneers"—those who pursue nontraditional occupations and who are more consistent (and more similar to men) in their career development paths. These women are, at present, atypical, yet their development in the professions does provide some important information, which will be examined more closely in the later section on professional women.

Job Characteristics

A great deal of debate has focused on what characteristics women expect or want from their jobs, and many of these debates have suggested contrasting patterns between women and men. It has been argued, for example, that men are generally more concerned with wages and with the opportunities for advancement that a job offers; women, in contrast, are thought to be more concerned with factors extrinsic to the job itself, such as the working conditions and the possibilities for social interaction (Herzberg, Mausn er, Peterson & Capwell, 1957). There have been studies that support this argument. For example, a national survey showed that women did value good hours and pleasant surroundings more than did men (Crowley, Levitan, & Quinn, 1973). Similarly, some surveys have indicated that women are more apt to value the social aspects of their jobs than are men.

A major problem with much of this earlier research is its failure to control for occupation and education. Thus comparisons of a female secretary to a male manager might indeed yield differences on an extrinsic-intrinsic dimension. However, when comparisons are made between males and females within the same occupational category, sex differences are generally not found. As one example, consider the factor of social interaction, which, it may be argued, is more characteristic of some secretarial jobs than it is of many other jobs. It may be the case that women, desiring social interaction in their work, seek out jobs that will satisfy that value. On the other hand, it is equally possible that women report valuing social interaction simply because it is a central feature of their job—more central than pay or challenge, perhaps. In support of this latter interpretation, studies that have controlled for the amount of interpersonal contact inherent in a job have found no sex differences in the value placed on this interaction (Nieva & Gutek, 1979).

The issue of expectations becomes important when we consider what women want from their work. If women do not realistically anticipate that they can have jobs with high pay, prestige, and responsibility, they may not focus their attention on these less-attainable aspects of a job. Instead, they may adjust to what is possible within the range of opportunities that appear to be available. Gurin (1981) has underlined the importance of expectations in the labor market experience of black and white women and men. In her study, white males thought their chances for employment were better and their abilities greater than did any of the other three groups. In addition, this group already had higher-paying jobs than did the other three groups.

By the same token, the employment expectancies of women were related to the actual labor market experiences that they had had. It is interesting to note that men, particularly white men, were more apt to have attempted to improve their position through job-related training or a change of work, while women were more apt to have sought educational supplements. Although both groups were thus exerting some effort to improve their situations, evidence indicated that the former strategy was the more successful one, accounting for some of the greater dissatisfaction among women.

Other evidence has shown that women have lower expectations than men, particularly in the area of pay. Major (Major & Konar, 1982; Major & McFarlin, 1982) reports that women will award themselves less money than men for an equivalent performance and will work longer for a set reward than will men. Further, women business students ask for a lower starting salary than men and make lower estimates of what other people are getting. Similar findings have been reported by Crosby (1982), who has studied the extent to which women feel deprived relative to other workers. In her study, women did not differ from men in satisfaction with their pay, even though the women were in actuality receiving significantly less. However, like men, their actual pay was reasonably congruent with their expectations. Perhaps pay is less important to women than it is to men. Alternatively, it may be that women have established their expectations in terms of the market prices. Thus for pay, as for social contact, values may be established in the context of what is reasonably available.

It is difficult to draw firm conclusions from this research without further investigation. Evidence that men and women have different values, priorities, and aspirations must inevitably be based on the status quo. To the extent that present opportunities and existent occupational structures differ greatly for women and men, it is difficult to state unequivocally what women would expect or want in a job if all possibilities were open.

Combining Work and Family

Because women traditionally have been invested with responsibility for taking care of the house and raising children, women who work outside the home are often faced with the issue of combining two roles in some manageable way. It is true, of course, that most men who work also have families and bear responsibilities for those families, yet the issue of combined roles for men has rarely been raised, at least not until very recently. In fact, the ways of combining roles have typically been conceptualized quite differently for women and men. Organizational theorists have suggested that working women are typically faced with simultaneous role demands, that require them to tend to household responsibilities at the same time that they are engaged in paid employment outside the home. Men are described as more apt to have sequential role demands, fulfilling one (often limited) role at home and a different role at work (Hall, 1972). From a slightly different perspective, Pleck (1977) has pointed to the "differential permeability" of boundaries between work and family roles for men and women. For women, the family role is allowed to intrude into the work role, as for example when the illness of a child compels the mother to be absent from work. When there is a clear choice between work and family, the woman has generally been expected to make the choice for family. For the man, Pleck argues, the work role is allowed to intrude into the family role. Thus it is more common for the man to bring home business colleagues for dinner, to bring work home from the office, or to expect the wife to make contacts in the community that are consistent with his work norms.

Although some of the role conflict models have been developed solely on the basis of white-collar experience, the pressure of simultaneous demands is very real for most wage-earning women who are married and/or have children. Given the rapid influx of married women into the labor market, the number of women who must deal with these issues is literally in the millions. Other women who face similar demands are those who are divorced or those who, in increasing numbers, are raising their children born out of wedlock. Thus in 1979 it was estimated that there were nearly twenty four million married women in the work force; of these, almost thirteen million had children under 18. In addition, close to three million women currently not married or with husbands absent and with one or more child dependents were also engaged in paid employment (U.S. Department of Labor, 1980). Both black and Puerto Rican women are more likely to be the head of household than are white women (Almquist & Wehrle-Einhorn, 1978). For all of these women, combining work and family is an issue that must be handled.

For the married woman, labor force participation has often been adapted to the demands of family life. Nieva and Gutek (1981) observe several forms that these adaptations may take. First, a woman may choose an intermittent work pattern, in which she works until she marries and then leaves the labor force, either to return when the children are older, to reenter only periodically for part-time work, or not to return at all. Another choice is to lower one's career commitment to jobs requiring less preparation time; still another choice is to select traditional jobs such as school teaching that may fit the household schedule more closely. Each of these choices increases the tendency for women to be relegated to sex-segregated, low-paying jobs in the labor force.

For the woman with children, whether married, unmarried, or divorced, employment decisions are often based on the availability of child care, either through established day-care centers or from relatives and friends. It has been estimated that as many as 90 percent of wage-earning mothers choose the latter arrangement, relying on relatives, siblings, or on individually paid workers (Moore & Sawhill, 1978). For the woman with low income, these decisions may be particularly difficult, since some alternatives may not be economically feasible for her.

The effects of family roles on women's employment are complex and multidetermined. Among the factors that need to be considered are the socioeconomic status, training, and education of the woman; the occupation and attitudes of the husband, if the woman is married; and the availability of support facilities that will make multiple roles easier. Relatively little research has been directed at these issues (Nieva & Gutek, 1981), but recent employment trends suggest that such research is needed.

Far more research effort has been devoted to examining the effect of women's work roles on their family lives, perhaps reflecting the traditional sense of priorities. Recently there has been a flurry of studies on the dual-career couple, documenting the problems and the resolutions that occur in this situation. Yet the recent emphasis on this professional model ignores the fact that among nonprofessional people, there is a long history of two people working out of economic necessity.

Much of the concern with husband-wife relations in dual-career couples has been with the division of labor within the household. In general, studies show that although employed women spend less time on household tasks than do full-time homemakers, the division of labor in the home is nowhere near equal. Men whose wives are also employed spend only slightly more time on household chores than do husbands of full-time homemakers. Housework is still defined as the woman's responsibility, whether she is a full-time homemaker or not. The difference is generally made up by the use of outside help, the purchase of services, and/or some lowering of standards within the house (Nieva & Gutek, 1981; Spence, Deaux, & Helmreich, in press).

Other investigations have focused on the relationship between husband and wife, in terms of power distribution and marital satisfaction. Generally, results show that the employed wife has greater power in family decisions than do full-time homemakers. This readjustment of the typical power differential is greatest among lower-class and working-class couples (Bahr, 1974). Findings regarding marital satisfaction are unclear, and appear to depend on additional factors such as both the husband's and wife's attitudes toward the wife working (Nieva & Gutek, 1981).

Despite substantial research, similar confusion remains concerning the effect that a woman's employment has on her children. Perhaps the only clear statement that can be made is that a mother who chooses to work does not inevitably create problems for her children (Hoffman, 1979). Among the numerous factors that have been documented as affecting this relationship are the attitudes of both husband (if present) and wife toward working, the quality of child-care arrangements, the amount of help received with housework, and the socioeconomic status of the woman (Moore & Sawhill, 1978).

Sexual Harassment

For many women (and for some men), sexual harassment is an unwanted component of their jobs. Although this problem undoubtedly has a long history, only recently has legal and social attention been devoted to it (Faley, 1982; MacKinnon, 1979). As defined by the federal government, "Sexual harassment is deliberate or repeated unsolicited verbal comments, gestures, or physical contact of a sexual nature that is considered to be unwelcome by the recipient" (Office of Personnel Management, 1980). MacKinnon (1979) has distinguished between two forms of sexual harassment. The first, termed *quid pro quo*, involves the proposal or actual exchange of sexual compliance for some employment opportunity, for example, being hired, getting a raise, or being promoted. The second and more insidious form of harassment occurs as a general condition of work. In this case, no specific exchanges are proposed, but unwanted sexual advances may occur in an almost casual fashion.

While scholars debate the technical definition of sexual harassment, popular opinion shows little more consensus as to what constitutes sexual harassment. When asked to evaluate "requests of sexual activity that would hurt the job situation if refused or help if it is accepted," 88 percent of male and 81 percent of female Los Angeles residents sampled defined this situation as sexual harassment. Even in this extreme case, some respondents did not see sexual harassment. In less clear-cut cases, the percentage of endorsement was substantially smaller. Thus when asked whether nonverbal behaviors of a sexual nature such as leering, touching, or brushing against another person was sexual harassment, 65 percent of the women but only 35 percent of the men agreed that it would be. Positive comments of a sexual nature were even less likely to be considered sexual harassment, endorsed by only 27 percent of the women and 11 percent of the men in this sample (Gutek, Nakamura, Gahart, Handschumacher, & Russell, 1980). Other studies have also found that women are more likely to consider a given behavior to be sexual harassment than are men (Tangri, 1982).

This lack of consensus as to what constitutes sexual harassment is one reason that awareness is often limited. There is little doubt that sexual harassment occurs, however. A survey of women employed at the United

Nations found that 49 percent believed that sexual pressure existed on their jobs (MacKinnon, 1979). In a Los Angeles survey, 11 percent of the women and 6 percent of the men reported that they had experienced *quid pro quo* requests for sexual activity; substantially more (approximately 46 percent of each sex) said that positive verbal comments of a sexual nature had been directed at them sometime in the past. In a recent, carefully controlled study, Johnson and Tangri (1981) sampled the civilian federal labor force, with a very high (85 percent) return rate on their questionnaires. In this sample of over 23,000 people, 42 percent of the women and 15 percent of the men reported experiencing sexual harassment within the preceding 24 months.

It is widely agreed that sexual harassment and power are intimately intertwined. In fact, the same behavior is more likely to be labeled sexual harassment when it is done by a supervisor than when done by a coworker (Tangri, 1982). This power differential generally places women at a disadvantage. As MacKinnon has observed, "Women employed in the paid labor force, typically hired 'as women,' dependent upon their income and lacking job alternatives, are particularly vulnerable to intimate violation in the form of sexual abuse at work" (MacKinnon, 1979, p. 1).

Gutek and Nakamura (1982) have speculated about the conditions that are most likely to contribute to sexual harassment. Among the factors they cite are the proximity of women and men in the workplace, the amount of power the potential victim has in the work environment, and the general atmosphere at work, including such factors as the explicit sexuality of dress. In addition, Gutek and Nakamura suggest that the percentage of women in a work group will also influence the occurrence of sexual harassment. It is the belief of these authors that sexual harassment toward women is most likely to occur either in jobs that are predominately female, where the female sex role may be an important component of the job, or in jobs that are predominately male, where men may test the responses of women in nontraditional settings.

Sexual harassment can be detrimental not only to the recipient but to the organization as well. For example, sexual harassment may lessen contact between women and men in a manner counter to work productivity (Gutek & Nakamura, 1982). More directly, some studies have shown that up to 17 percent of women have quit a job because of sexual harassment; an additional 7 percent have reported missing work because of such incidents. For the individual woman, sexual harassment may impede progress, lower self-confidence, and reduce career commitment (Gutek & Nakamura, 1982). Although difficult to assess and document, sexual harassment is a serious issue at both the individual and the organizational level.

The issues discussed in the preceding pages cut across occupational boundaries. Yet the psychological and social factors affecting women in various broad occupational groups are in some cases quite different, and may evidence unique demands and problems. Consequently, it is important to analyze these different groups of wage-earning women, categorized here for convenience as white-collar, pink-collar and blue-collar jobs.

WHITE-COLLAR WOMEN

Although "white-collar" is a convenient label, the contents of that category are in fact quite diverse, consisting of at least three distinct classes of workers: women in traditionally male professional fields; women in traditionally female professional fields; and women in lower-status clerical jobs. Nearly two-thirds of all working women are in one of these three categories, with the highest percentage in the clerical group. The smallest percentage is in the first category—women in male professions—although recent research has tended to focus disproportionately on this group of women.

The factors that influence a woman to choose a traditionally male profession have been the topic of many investigations. Although the results of these studies are not always consistent, a variety of factors have been implicated. Mothers may be influential, with professional women most likely to have mothers who were either satisfied career women *or* unhappy housewives. Other factors identified as important are a strong identification with the father, a high need for achievement and the intellectual aptitude to accomplish these needs, and support from faculty and significant others (Nieva & Gutek, 1981). In some cases, career decisions have been made relatively late. For example, jobs that began in a more traditional secretarial mold may have developed into managerial positions (Hennig & Jardim, 1976).

Even within nontraditional fields, there is often some occupational segregation. In medicine and law there is a tendency for women to select certain specialties, for example, pediatrics and divorce law, that are seemingly more consistent with the female stereotype (Patterson & Engelberg, 1978).

Women entering traditionally male fields inevitably encounter some discrimination, in part by virtue of the fact that they are simply different from the norm (Kanter, 1977). Tokens, to use Kanter's term, have higher visibility and will hence garner more attention. Their differences from the predominant group members are exaggerated, and their own qualities may be distorted to fit a prevailing stereotype. Typically, women in male fields report some problems with their peers, and they may feel that their opportunities for advancement are less clear than they are for men (Kanter, 1977; U. S. Department of Labor, 1978). On the other hand, job satisfaction for women in these positions is typically high, and the women point to challenge, responsibility, pay, and status as positive features of their jobs.

Women who enter traditionally female professions, for example, nursing, elementary education, and social work, do not face the same kinds of discriminatory pressures. At the same time, such female-dominated fields are usually lower in pay and prestige. Typically, these professions are more flexible in terms of entry and exit. Somewhat less education may be required, regulations and licensing may be less formalized, and a person may be able to reenter the market more easily after a period of absence (Grimm, 1978). Such characteristics make the jobs more appealing for the woman who seeks a job that will be compatible with a husband's job (Nieva & Gutek, 1981).

It has been suggested by some writers that women entering traditionally female fields have a weaker career commitment than do those women who choose male-dominated fields. Although that is a possible explanation, it also seems likely that the greater accessibility of female fields makes them more attractive or more feasible for many women. Among black women, movement into these female-dominated professions has been particularly strong. For example, although 61 percent of black professionals were female in 1970, the majority of the women were found in fields such as social work and education rather than medicine and law (Almquist & Wehrle-Einhorn, 1978).

At the bottom of the white-collar ladder are the clerical jobs that employ more than a third of all female workers. These jobs are almost entirely held by women. More particularly, they have traditionally been the province of white women, although black women are increasingly entering these fields (Allen, 1979). Pay is typically low, and opportunities for advancement are severely restricted in most cases. Positive job characteristics most often mentioned by clerical women are the interpersonal aspects; negative features often include resentment of doing personal favors and "non-professional" tasks (Kanter, 1977).

In summary, it is difficult to talk about a single type of white-collar woman. The range of jobs within this general classification is considerable, covering the highest-paid and some of the lowest-paid women workers, including some of the most typical and some of the least typical fields for females, and varying in job characteristics from challenging to routine, from intrinsic to extrinsic, and from as long-term as a career commitment to as short-term as the transient secretarial services.

PINK-COLLAR WOMEN

Pink-collar work is a term that has been applied to a cluster of jobs that are primarily held by women, among them sales clerk, beautician, waitress, and domestic servant (Howe, 1977). In 1980, 17 percent of all women were employed in service jobs; another 7 percent were sales workers, and an additional 2½ percent were domestic servants (U. S. Department of Labor, January 1981). Among black and other minority women these numbers were generally higher: 24 percent were employed in some type of service job, 3 percent were in sales, and 6½ percent were domestic servants.

Often the women who enter these jobs do not plan to work full-time, nor do they intend to stay in these jobs for an indefinite period of time (Baker, 1978). Rather, the jobs are often viewed as part-time or temporary work, something to augment the paycheck until personal conditions have changed. Entry into these jobs is relatively easy, given a reasonably robust economy, because the requirements are often minimal. For many of these jobs, little or no training is required. At the same time, these jobs offer limited rewards. The pay is typically low, there is generally little chance for advancement, and there may be little recognition for the women who perform the jobs (Howe, 1977).

Domestic workers present a particularly limiting area of employment. Women in domestic service are more often older and are more often black, and their earnings are among the lowest of all women workers (Katzman, 1978). Furthermore, the isolation of these women, typically the lone worker in a household, does not allow them contact or comparison with other workers. They are, it has been argued, virtually powerless, covered by no formal structures, typically without fringe benefits or job security, and subject to the whims of a single employer (Katzman, 1978). Pink-collar women have been ignored by most social scientists. Apart from the descriptive account of Howe (1977), little research attention has been paid to the women in this particularly female ghetto.

BLUE-COLLAR WOMEN

In 1980, nearly 14 percent of employed women were in blue-collar occupations. Among black and minority women, this figure was somewhat higher at 17.7 percent; for whites it was a slightly lower 13.2 percent. The majority of these women are in operative or semiskilled jobs, while less than 2 percent are in the higher-paying skilled craft jobs. Many of these women are employed in the traditionally female fields of textiles and garments, following the pattern set in Lowell more than 100 years ago. Increasingly, however, women are entering the traditionally male blue-collar fields, moving into apprentice programs, and earning the up-to-$25 per hour pay that male blue-collar workers may enjoy.

The backgrounds of these women are diverse. Baker (1978) has reported that women in blue-collar jobs tend to be from working-class families, often have less than a high school education, and are often married to working-class men with similar jobs. In contrast, Walshok's (1981) study of women in traditionally male, skilled and semiskilled jobs found that more than half of the women had some college education, and more than 25 percent were college graduates. In part, this discrepancy may reflect a difference between women entering traditionally female and traditionally male blue-collar fields. It may also reflect the uncertain state of knowledge in this area, where few investigations have been conducted and samples have tended to be opportunistic rather than systematic.

Most wage-earning women do not directly enter blue-collar jobs, particularly not those in the traditionally male sectors, and most have not systematically planned to engage in this kind of work. Typically, women in these jobs have previously held clerical or service jobs more typical for women (U. S. Department of Labor, 1978; Walshok, 1981). For white women, clerical jobs are a more common background; for black women, service and low-level factory jobs are more typical precedents (Walshok, 1981). Movement from the more traditionally female, lower-paying jobs into the higher-paying blue-collar jobs is often a matter of opportunity and on-the-job experience. As Walshok notes, "Most of the women did not plan their careers. Rather, they moved from job to job as opportunities presented themselves and most frequently discovered interests and capacities along the way" (1981, p. 116). Thus for these women, work was a necessity, and initial jobs were taken on the basis of availability rather than as a result of career planning. In the course of their work history, certain opportunities may have presented themselves—often in the form of special programs or outreach attempts for women. Many of these women already knew what kind of work they didn't want to do (often including the traditionally female jobs that they had), but they were less certain what they did want to do. Special programs and opportunities often crystalized the answers, providing the context for realization of the job qualities that the women were seeking (Walshok, 1981).

What kind of factors are valued by women in blue-collar jobs? Money is clearly one important aspect (Baker, 1978; O'Farrell & Harlan, 1980; U. S. Department of Labor, 1978; Walshok, 1981), reflecting the fact that blue-collar jobs are often better paying than traditionally female jobs. Such findings, of course, provide evidence that challenges the assumption that women value such factors less than do men. Other characteristics often mentioned as important for women in blue-collar jobs are challenge, variety, and accomplishment (Walshok, 1981; U. S. Department of Labor,

1978). The available evidence suggests that the majority of women in blue-collar work, particularly those in skilled and semiskilled jobs, are highly satisfied with their jobs, with advantages far outweighing any perceived disadvantages.

This is not to say that women in blue-collar jobs do not see any negative factors. In a study of women in blue-collar jobs in the utilities field, Myers and Lee (U. S. Department of Labor, 1978) reported that a number of women disliked the dirty work, outside environments, and some mechanical aspects of their jobs. Approximately one-third of blue-collar women surveyed have reported some hostility or harassment (not necessarily sexual) from their male coworkers (O'Farrell & Harlan, 1980; U. S. Department of Labor, 1978).

Walshok (1981) found that approximately one-third of the women in her study had at some time encountered actual sexual harassment. A similar figure emerged in a recent study of women auto workers (Bjorn & Gruber, 1981). These accounts of sexual harassment are not evenly distributed across female blue-collar workers. Younger women report more frequent harassment than do older women; single and divorced women report more than married women. The severity of the harassment is reported to be greater among women with less than two years seniority, suggesting a "hazing" effect. Although black women do not report a greater frequency of harassment, their reported incidents tend to be more severe (Gruber & Bjorn, 1981). Of further interest is the report that more than 25 percent of the harassment incidents described by women auto workers were initiated by a foreman, despite the fact that supervisors comprised only 5 percent of the males in that plant (Gruber & Bjorn, 1981). Such a pattern is consistent with the thesis that power differentials are more common in cases of sexual harassment.

Although these numbers are substantial, Walshok (1981) suggests that sexual harassment is less widespread in the blue-collar world than in some other employment settings, and data on reported incidents would support this suggestion. One explanation is that the blue-collar environment may place more stress on work relationships than on traditional male-female roles. In a hard hat, protective goggles, and safety boots, it is, after all, not as easy to distinguish male and female nor for sex-associated characteristics to be salient. Further (with the exception of the foreman), the power differentials between men and women are often less, as both are typically performing similar jobs. The apparently lower frequency of sexual harassment could also reflect the fact that it may be easier for women to deal with the issue directly, with "straight talk" and even verbal aggressiveness more readily accepted in a blue-collar setting (Walshok, 1981). Union protection may also be a factor in limiting the incidence of sexual harassment in blue-collar occupations.

Despite these problems, not to be minimized, the majority of blue-collar women report positive relations with their fellow employees. Many report that men do not resent them, and many others say that although there was initial resentment, it dissipated over time (Department of Labor, 1978; Bjorn & Gruber, 1981; Walshok, 1981). In general, the strategies for success reported in the available studies are remarkably similar, stressing perseverence, hard work, learning the job, and adapting to the norms of the work group (U. S. Department of Labor, 1978; Walshok, 1981). Thus the women who have been successful tend to focus on the job rather than on the interpersonal environment, and make internal attributions for their own success.

Considerably less is known as to how women in blue-collar jobs integrate their work and home life. Scattered reports suggest that some husbands may disapprove of the woman working in a predominately male environment. Working different hours may make coordination between husband and wife difficult, and arrangements for child care may pose problems for the woman whose work schedule does not fit a nine-to-five pattern. At the same time, many of the blue-collar women that have been interviewed do not report great conflicts between their roles as worker and mother (Walshok, 1981), suggesting that both perceptions of the problem and satisfactory solutions may be different for the blue-collar woman than for her white-collar or professional counterpart (Walshok, 1981).

In summary, available information about blue-collar women, although not extensive, suggests a picture rather different from that of the woman employed in traditionally female fields. Although initial job choices may not differ much from those of women who remain in traditionally female fields, the current situation is quite different. How typical the results from these early studies are remains to be determined. With the women of steel, we will extend the investigations one step further.

3

Legislation and Public Policy Affecting Women at Work

Throughout most of its history, the legal system of the United States has treated women as unique. As noted by Herma Hill Kay, "The notion that men and women stand as equals before the law was not the original understanding" (1981, p. 1). Nor was it the understanding nearly 100 years after the Declaration of Independence, when Myra Bradwell attempted to practice law. Denied a license by the Illinois Supreme Court because she was a woman, Bradwell appealed to the U. S. Supreme Court. They upheld the Illinois decision, noting that "the paramount of destiny and mission of woman are to fulfill the noble and benign offices of wife and mother," and invoking "the law of the Creator" (quoted in Kay, 1981, pp. 4–5).

Whether propelled by divine guidance or human judgment, the laws of the United States have, until quite recently, treated women as a special category. With regard to employment, so-called "protective legislation" actually constrained women's right to work. In the 1960s and 1970s, particularly after the passage of the Civil Rights Act of 1964, legal views of women began to change. In recent years, the law has tended to protect women's rights to work, and numerous pieces of legislation that constrained this right have been overturned. Most recently, women's right to work free from harassment based on their gender has been increasingly supported by law. In this chapter we will provide a general overview of legislative and judicial actions that have affected the employment of women, tracing their evolution from constrainer to protector of women's rights to work outside the home.[1]

THE DEVELOPMENT OF PROTECTIVE LEGISLATION

As early as 1827, workers in some parts of the United States were suggesting a ten-hour day (Kessler-Harris, 1982). These requests were not specific to women, but rather represented a broader-based attempt by workers to increase their bargaining position. These efforts enjoyed some success. President Van Buren issued an executive order in 1840 mandating a ten-hour work day for federal employees. The state governments of Ohio and Wisconsin followed suit for their employees in 1857, and a number of other states determined that ten-hour work periods would be standard unless a contract specified otherwise. Efforts to reduce the work day continued to be mounted during the latter half of the nineteenth century. By 1871, for example, the Knights of Labor were demanding an eight-hour day (Kessler-Harris, 1982).

Despite some success, the move for a shorter working day met considerable resistance as well. In 1905, the forces of resistance won when the U. S. Supreme Court declared a New York law limiting working hours to be invalid. In this case, involving bakers, the court stated, "Clean, and wholesome bread does not depend upon whether a baker works but 10 hours per day" (Kessler-Harris, 1982, p. 183).

Although a general reduction of working hours for all workers was not initially successful, protective labor legislation for women was accepted much more readily. State laws providing special restrictions or benefits for employed women were enacted to alleviate the poor working conditions and long hours to which women were subjected. The focus of the legislation was to protect the woman for her role as a wife and mother, thereby insuring the welfare of the family unit.

At least three different kinds of legislation that restricted the work sphere of women were enacted during the nineteenth and early twentieth centuries: limitations on the kinds of work, limitations on the number of hours, and stipulations regarding minimum wages.

Kinds of Work

Restrictions on the kinds of work that women might perform typically focused on either the physical or the moral aspects of the job. The widely held belief about women's physical incapacity was the impetus for protective laws dealing with the amount of weight a woman could lift on the job. Other jobs were proscribed for women on the grounds that such jobs would expose women to indecency. Jobs such as bartenders, telegraph messengers, wrestlers, and miners, for example, were viewed as "unladylike"; jobs requiring night work would unreasonably confront women with undesirable elements in society.

The situation involving iron molders in New York provides one clear and relevant example of this movement. As early as 1894, some women had worked in the foundries making "cores," and their numbers continued to increase. In 1907, male union members began to protest their presence, pointing both to the incompatability of the factories with women's "finer nature" and the presumably lower work standards that women would accept as compared to men. Fines were levied against union members who were caught instructing women, and expulsion was recommended for a second offense. These internal actions were followed by an appeal to the state commission in 1910. The commission, while acknowledging that the working conditions were generally bad for everyone, observed that "it would have been far better if women had never been originally allowed to enter this employment" (quoted in Kessler-Harris, 1982, p. 204). And while they did not favor immediate dismissal of the female employees, they did suggest that future work by women in the core rooms should be suppressed. Subsequently, legislative action prohibited women from working in the same rooms as men and from certain locations, regulated weight limits for women, and effectively eliminated women from the foundries (Kessler-Harris, 1982).

Although not the explicit intent of such legislation, exclusion of women from certain jobs inevitably meant that men would dominate in those occupations. Options for women were thus limited. Even more important and damaging was the continued belief in an implied inferiority. Protective legislation, rather than discriminating in favor of women, discriminated against women in the work place.

Maximum Hours

The first maximum-hour law specifically directed toward women was passed in Ohio in 1852, and limited work to ten hours per day. Three other states passed similar restrictions shortly after the Civil War. In 1890, Massachusetts passed laws against night work for women.

The American Association for Labor Legislation, the National Consumer's League, under Florence Kelley, and the Women's Trade Union, under Rose Scheiderman played central roles in the passage of ten-hour and eight-hour limitations for working women. They argued that long hours would damage a woman's health. "A woman's body is unable to withstand strain, fatigue and privations as well as a man's. The nervous strain resulting from monotonous work and speeding up, intensified by the piece work system, when coupled with excessive length of working hours, can only result in undermining the whole physical structure of the woman. . . . (It) can destroy the health of women and render them unfit to perform their functions as mothers" (State of New York, Factory Investigating Commission, quoted in Dye, 1980, p. 145).

The Pennsylvania Superior Court concurred with these sentiments in an 1896 decision upholding limited work weeks for women. In their opinion, "Adult females are a class as distinct as minors, separated by natural conditions from all other laborers, and are so constituted as to be unable to endure physical exertion and exposure to the extent and degree that is not harmful to adult workers" (Kessler-Harris, 1982, p. 186). Thus women were quite explicitly considered on a par with children. Just as children are protected by the state, so were women viewed as needing the paternal power of the state to protect them from undesirable work.

Fifty-six years after the first maximum hours legislation, Oregon's ten-hour law for women in industry was upheld by the United States Supreme Court (*Muller* versus *Oregon*). Arguing this case in 1908, Louis Brandeis and his sister-in-law Josephine Goldmark described a variety of consequences for the woman who had to work longer hours. This bleak picture included physical debility, laxity of moral fibre, vertigo, constipation, varicose veins, and displacement of the uterus (Kessler-Harris, 1982). Both physical weakness and maternal duties were invoked to support the protective legislation. The Court was convinced, and agreed that sex is a valid basis for classification. As they stated in their opinion, "She is properly placed in a class by herself, and legislation designed for her protection may be sustained, even when like legislation is not necessary for men and could not be sustained" (quoted in Rawalt, 1973, p. 5). Thus treatment of all women as a class was not seen as a denial of equal protection of the law.

The Muller decision precipitated the enactment of similar maximum hour laws in other states. By 1913, when the United States Department of Labor was formed, 27 states had some form of maximum hours restrictions on the employment of women. By 1967, 41 states and the District of Columbia had maximum daily or weekly hours laws for women in one or more occupations or industries. Table 3.1 shows the chronological development of state hour laws for women from 1913 to 1967.

Often included in these state statutes were rules pertaining to days of rest, meal and rest periods, and night work. Thus in a 1967 assessment, the Department of Labor reported that nearly half of the states had a six-day week for women in some or all industries. Twenty states either prohibited employment for women at night, set maximum hour standards different from those of day work, or regulated the conditions under which women could work after specified evening hours. Some states prohibited night work only in certain industries or occupations. For example, in North Dakota and Washington, the prohibition applied to elevator operators; in Ohio, to taxicab drivers. Utah forbid the employment of women in

TABLE 3.1 Chronological Development of State Hour Laws for Women, March 1967

A. Daily Maximum Hour Laws[a]

		Number of Jurisdictions with—						
		Daily Maximum Hours of—						
Year	Laws	8 or less	Over 8, Less Than 9	9	Over 9, Less Than 10	10	Over 10	No Law
1913	27	3		4	1	19		25
1920	43	10	1	13		15	4	9
1940	44	19	1	14		8	2	8
1950	43	18	1	13		11		9
1960	43	18	1	13		11		9
1967	42	18	1	12		11		10

B. Weekly Maximum Hour Laws[a]

		Number of Jurisdictions with—							
		Weekly Maximum Hours of—							
Year	Laws	44	45	48	50	54	Over 54, Less Than 58	58 and 60	No Law
1913	22			1		6	2	13	30
1920	37			8	1	12	8	8	15
1940	42	2	2	19	2	10	2	5	10
1950	41	1		21	4	8	2	5	11
1960	41	1		22	4	8	2	4	11
1967	41	1		23	4	8	1	4	11

restaurants after midnight. Arizona and the District of Columbia did not allow women under 21 to do night messenger service (U. S. Department of Labor, 1967). Table 3.2 traces the enactment of legislation governing women's maximum hours, day of rest, meal and rest periods, and night work from 1913 to 1967.

TABLE 3.1 *(continued)*

C. Jurisdictions with Laws Governing—

Year	Day of Rest	Lunch Period	Rest Period	Night Work[b]
1913	1	6		7
1920	14	20	4	17
1940	24	27	4	19
1950	23	29	8	18
1960	23	27	12	22
1967	23	25	13	21

[a]The highest standard (fewest maximum hours) shown, applicable to one or more industries. A few of these laws also apply to men.

[b]Exclusive of night-work laws applicable to females under 21 years of age.

Source: Reprinted from *Growth of Labor Law in the United States,* The United States Department of Labor, 1967, p. 127.

Minimum Wages

Minimum wage legislation, the subject of considerable constitutional litigation, was different from maximum hour laws. Hours laws could be applied to women on the basis of biological assumptions, but there was no physiological reason for women to earn a specified wage. Minimum wage legislation first became a major public policy issue during the early 1900s, a period of social and economic change in the United States. Numerous studies by various social reform organizations and government commissions brought the plight of the average family to public attention. In many families it was necessary for the wife and even the children to supplement the wages of the family head. Exploitation of women and children in factories and mines was prevalent. Although both men and women had inadequate wages, women's wages were generally lower. Further, some companies had established a precedent by raising women's wages to compensate for their shorter hours. Thus in the early 1900s, minimum wage legislation was directed primarily at women and children.

The first minimum wage law for women and children was adopted in Massachusetts in 1912. The only enforcement the bill carried was a promise to publish the names of noncomplying employers in the newspaper. Eight additional states passed similar legislation the following year, but again adequate enforcement was not established.

Opponents of the minimum wage laws were numerous and active.

TABLE 3.2 Jurisdictions with Hour Laws for Women in 1913 and March 1967

State	Daily Hours 1913	Daily Hours 1967	Weekly Hours 1913	Weekly Hours 1967	Day of Rest 1913	Day of Rest 1967	Lunch Period 1913	Lunch Period 1967	Rest Period 1913	Rest Period 1967	Night Work 1913	Night Work 1967
Total	27	42	22	41	1	23	6	25		13	7	21
Alabama												
Alaska										X		
Arizona		X		X		X				X		
Arkansas		X				X		X				
California	X	X	X	X		X		X		X		X
Colorado	X	X		X		X		X		X		
Connecticut	X	X	X	X		X		X			X	X
Delaware												
District of Columbia		X		X		X		X				
Florida												
Georgia		X		X								
Hawaii												
Idaho		X		X								
Illinois	X	X		X		X						X
Indiana								X			X	
Iowa												
Kansas		X		X		X		X				X
Kentucky	X	X	X	X						X		
Louisiana	X	X	X	X		X	X	X				
Maine	X	X	X	X				X				
Maryland	X	X	X	X			X	X			X	X
Massachusetts	X	X	X	X			X	X			X	X
Michigan	X	X	X	X		X		X				X

42

State													
Minnesota	X					X							X
Mississippi	X	X	X		X								X
Missouri	X		X		X								X
Montana	X		X		X								
Nebraska	X		X		X					X	X	X	X
Nevada	X		X		X					X		X	X
New Hampshire	X	X	X		X			X		X	X		X
New Jersey	X	X	X	X	X	X		X		X	X		X
New Mexico	X		X		X	X				X			X
New York	X		X		X			X		X	X		X
North Carolina	X		X		X			X		X	X		X
North Dakota	X		X		X			X		X	X		X
Ohio	X		X		X		X	X		X		X	X
Oklahoma	X				X			X		X			
Oregon	X		X		X			X		X	X	X	X
Pennsylvania	X		X		X			X		X	X	X	X
Puerto Rico	X		X		X					X		X	X
Rhode Island	X		X		X			X		X			X
South Carolina	X		X		X			X					X
South Dakota	X		X		X							X	
Tennessee	X		X		X								
Texas	X				X								
Utah	X		X		X			X		X		X	X
Vermont	X		X		X								
Virginia	X		X		X								
Washington	X		X		X			X		X		X	X
West Virginia	X				X					X			
Wisconsin	X		X		X		X	X		X		X	X
Wyoming	X		X		X			X		X		X	X

Source: U.S. Department of Labor, 1967, pp. 128–129.

Citing the traditional "laissez-faire" economic policy of letting the market set the wage rate, they argued that minimum wage laws violated the rights of employers and employees to freedom of contract. Suits were brought in Oregon, Arkansas, Massachusetts, Minnesota, and Washington, but in each case the law was declared constitutional. Proponents of the laws felt vindicated in their belief that women and children would be exploited if it were not for these laws.

However, in 1923 the United States Supreme Court reversed itself and ruled that the District of Columbia's minimum wage law was unconstitutional. In the case of *Adkins* v. *Children's Hospital*, a woman elevator operator was discharged by her employer, who refused to pay the required minimum wage. A man who was willing to work for less—and not being covered by the law, was able to do so—was hired in her place. As the Court explained in its ruling, "It is quite simply and exclusively a price fixing law, confined to adult women . . . who are legally as capable of contracting for themselves as men" (Kessler-Harris, 1982, p. 198). Following this decision, the laws of several states were declared unconstitutional, while others went unenforced due to a lack of appropriations.

Despite the Supreme Court's decision on the Adkins case, the poverty and low wages associated with the depression of the 1930s renewed interest in minimum wage legislation. The issue was not finally resolved until 1937 when the Supreme Court reversed its Adkins decision and upheld the constitutionality of a minimum wage law in the state of Washington (*West Coast Hotel* v. *Parrish*). The following excerpt from the majority opinion is particularly reflective of feelings at the time:

> There is an additional and compelling consideration which recent economic experience has brought into a strong light. The exploitation of a class of workers who are in an unequal position . . . is not only detrimental to their health and well-being but casts a direct burden for their support upon the community. What these workers lose in wages the taxpayers are called upon to pay. The bare cost of living must be met. (quoted in U. S. Department of Labor, 1967, p. 83)

In light of this decision, laws that had previously been declared unconstitutional were reexamined. Some were declared valid, while others passed in a revised form. by 1938, 22 states, the District of Columbia, and Puerto Rico had minimum wage laws. Some of these minimum wage statutes also included regulations requiring a premium rate for overtime.

There were other protective legislation bills as well. For example, a 1913 Women's Labor Law not only regulated hours and conditions of employment, but also dealt with such features as the intervals between work periods, suitable facilities for seating females, washrooms, dressing rooms, lavatories, lunch rooms, and drinking water. In each case, sharper restrictions were placed on the work of women than of men.

OPPOSITION TO PROTECTIVE LABOR LAWS

The majority of organized women's groups initially advocated protective legislation, seeing it as being in the best interest of women. Yet some women, most notably members of the National Women's Party, did not want the restrictions on night work, overtime, and weight lifting to apply to them, and saw the contradictions involved in seeking equality without equal footing. Opposition by working women grew during World War I. During this period, thousands of women took men's places in the work force. Women were hired as telegraph messengers, elevator operators, letter carriers, ticket collectors, and numerous other jobs that had been held previously by men.

In New York City women sought higher-paying transit system jobs. As a subway ticket collector, guard, or conductor, a woman could earn $20 to $25 a week—this at a time when more than 60 percent of the city's female workers earned less than $14, and only 8 percent earned more than $20 (Dye, 1980). The Women's Trade Union League sought to have state labor laws regulating hours and night work extended. Whereas these "protective" restrictions had covered only industrial and mercantile establishments, the League wanted coverage for elevator operators and transit women as well. The legislature responded with the Lockwood Transportation Act, which extended the protective laws to female transit employees. Immediately, the Brooklyn Rapid Transit Company dismissed nearly 1500 women guards, conductors, and ticket agents and replaced them with men (Dye, 1980).

These dismissed women became vigorous opponents of protective statutes that affected only women, having experienced the consequences of so-called protection. Women in the printing trades, another traditionally male occupation, also opposed the protective laws, believing that prohibition of night work would put them at a disadvantage to the men. A major lobbying force in support of these groups was the National Women's Party (NWP), a wing of the women's suffrage movement. The NWP reasoned that the statutes were essentially discriminatory, reinforcing women's inferior social and economic status. As one member of the party explained, "If . . . a law is passed applying to women and not applying to men, it will discriminate against women and handicap them in competing with men in earning their livelihood" (Kessler-Harris, 1982, p. 206).

Debates about protective legislation became part of the larger debate about an equal rights amendment, the so-called blanket amendment that proposed equal rights for men and women in all areas. Then, as has been true nearly 60 years later, the debate was fierce. The proposed Constitutional amendment did not pass, and protective legislation remained in effect for a number of years to come.

In 1948, the United States Supreme Court affirmed the concept of protective legislation, using a principle of "any rational basis." In the *Goesart* v. *Cleary* case, the Court upheld a Michigan statute that denies a bartender's license to a woman "unless she be wife or daughter of the male owner" (Kanowitz, 1969). Not only did the Court decide that this statute was not in violation of the Equal Protection Clause of the Fourteenth Amendment; but they proposed in addition "any rational basis" as the test for equal protection purposes. As Justice Frankfurter stated, "Since the line [the legislators] have drawn *is not without a basis in reason*, we cannot give ear to the suggestions that the real impulse behind this legislation was an unchivalrous desire for male bartenders to monopolize the calling" (Kanowitz, 1969). This line of argument served as a ready defense for statutes that imposed weight limitations or that barred women from certain occupations.

The passage of Title VII of the Civil Rights Act of 1964 signaled a major change. While Title VII prohibited discrimination in employment on the basis of sex, state protective labor legislation required different treatment of individuals on the basis of their sex. Was observance of the state laws in conflict with Title VII? Advocates of the state laws argued that no real conflict existed, contending that Congress had not intended to strike down such laws but only those that denied equality of opportunity to women. Opponents countered that the state laws were discriminatory. The Equal Employment Opportunity Commission followed a somewhat uneven path in dealing with this issue until 1969 when it issued revised guidelines on sex discrimination, stating:

1. Many States have enacted laws or promulgated administrative regulations with respect to the employment of females. Among these laws are those which prohibit or limit the employment of females, e.g., the employment of females in certain occupations, in jobs requiring the lifting or carrying of weights exceeding certain prescribed limits, during certain hours of the night, or for more than a specified number of hours per day or per week.

2. The Commission believes that such State laws and regulations, although originally promulgated for the purpose of protecting females, have ceased to be relevant to our technology or to the expanding role of the female worker in our economy. The Commission has found that such laws and regulations do not take into account the capacities, preferences, and abilities of individual females and tend to discriminate rather than protect. Accordingly, the Commission has concluded that such laws and regulations conflict with Title VII of the Civil Rights Act of 1964 and will

not be considered a defense to an otherwise established unlawful employment practice or as a basis for the application of the bona fide occupational qualification exception. (U. S. Department of Labor, 1973, p. 10)

A frenzy of litigation under Title VII followed, with an almost perfect record of decisions by federal courts outlawing sex-based laws as a violation of Title VII and the Supremacy Clause of the Constitution. Women workers in trade unions were some of the first to institute suits. At their own expense, they challenged laws restricting hour laws, weight-lifting limitations, and separate seniority lists, as violations of Title VII. Some typical cases involving sex discrimination under the guise of protective legislation are summarized in Table 3.3.

State protective labor laws for women were essentially laid to rest in the late 1960s and early 1970s by repeals and amendments of state laws, state and federal administrative rulings, or court decisions. Today, it is clear that both the concept and the statutes of women's protective legislation limited economic opportunities for women and reinforced stereotypical notions of women as weak, dependent, vulnerable, and maternal. The legislation originally passed to protect women had actually limited economic opportunities, and thus worked against many women.

THE ERA OF EQUAL EMPLOYMENT RIGHTS

In the past 20 years, the federal government has taken a more active role in expanding women's economic opportunities, in large part as a response to the active women's movement. These developments have been associated with, and in many respects are parallel to, the struggle for equal employment rights for racial minorities.

The federal government has taken an implicit interest in assuring equal employment opportunities for racial minorities since June of 1941 when President Franklin D. Roosevelt created the Fair Employment Practices Committee (Executive Order 8802). This order applied to all defense contractors and vocational-training programs that were administered by federal agencies. For both employers and labor unions, it imposed an obligation to provide for full and equitable participation of all workers, without discrimination, in defense industries. Similar committees and Executive Orders were promulgated by Presidents Truman and Eisenhower during the next 25 years.

In 1961, President John F. Kennedy issued Executive Order 10925, which included two significant provisions with regard to minority hiring. First, contractors were required "to take affirmative action to insure that

TABLE 3.3   A Sample of Court Cases Dealing with Protective Legislation

Weeks v. *Southern Bell Telephone and Telegraph Company* (1969):

The lower court in this case upheld the employer's refusal to hire a woman as switchman. His argument was based on a state law that limited women to lifting a maximum of 30 pounds. The appellate court reversed this decision, invoking the Supremacy Clause of the Constitution. They held that the employer failed to prove that sex was a bona fide occupational qualification for the switchman position. In another issue, the court stated that women could not be rejected because a job required emergency callouts after midnight.

Sailer Inn, Inc. v. *Kirby* (1971):

A California law prohibited women from tending bar unless they or their husbands held a liquor license. The Supreme Court of California found this law in conflict with the 1964 Civil Rights Act making it unlawful to deprive persons of employment opportunities on the basis of sex.

Manning v. *General Motors Corp.* (1971):

Protective laws in the state of Ohio excluded women from working more than a 48-hour week and from lifting weights in excess of 25 pounds, and required the company to furnish seats to female employees when they were not engaged in active duties. These laws were ruled invalid, in violation of the 1964 Civil Rights Act.

Richards v. *Griffith Rubber Mills* (1969):

The court held that Title VII superseded an Oregon order regulating the weights that female workers were permitted to lift.

Bowe v. *Colgate-Palmolive Co.* (1969):

This case involved a protective practice instituted by an employer rather than a state law. The employer was alleged to be in violation of Title VII by not accepting bids from women for jobs that required lifting more than 35 pounds. Although the lower court upheld the practice, the finding was reversed by the appellate court. The latter court stated that if weight-lifting conditions were applied, they must be applied to all workers regardless of sex.

Homemakers, Inc. of Los Angeles v. *Division of Industrial Welfare* (1973):

Extra benefits for women, specifically overtime pay requirements, were ruled unlawfully discriminatory against men.

Rosenfelt v. *Southern Pacific Co.* (1971):

A state law that banned female employment in jobs that required the lifting of heavy objects was found in conflict with the federal ban on sex discrimination. The court ruled that such laws deny employment opportunities on the basis of stereotyped characterizations of the physical capabilities and endurance of women.

applicants are employed, and that employees are treated during employment without regard to their race, creed, color or national origin" (Jones, 1976, p. 175). Second, sanctions could be imposed for violation of these contractual obligations. As Jones has observed, "By far the most important contribution of the Kennedy Executive Order was the creative utilization of affirmative action, a remedial concept usually imposed (only) after determination of guilt, as a requirement for doing business with the government" (Jones, 1976, p. 175). During the first five years after the Kennedy order, the voluntary approach prevailed. Hence, the affirmative action approach "gathered dust" (Jones, 1976, p. 176).

The Equal Pay Act of 1963 was the first legal recognition of sex discrimination in the employment setting. Although not dealing with any employment issues other than compensation, it nonetheless marked an important shift in legislative attitudes towards working women (Greenberger, 1980). Of greater consequence for women's entrance into traditionally male-dominated occupations is the Civil Rights Act of 1964 and its subsequent amendments.

Title VII of the 1964 Civil Rights Act prohibits discrimination in employment on the basis of race, color, sex, religion, or national origin. The inclusion of sex in this act was not the product of thoughtful debate. Indeed, the amendment adding sex to the coverage was passed only one day before Title VII was approved, and was introduced by a Virginia Congressman who had opposed the act as a whole. Some accused him of attempting to sabotage the act by including sex in the coverage (Kay, 1981). Nonetheless, sex is part of Title VII coverage and the Act has been the major foundation for subsequent action dealing with equal opportunity in employment for women (Greenberger, 1980).

In 1965, President Lyndon Johnson issued Executive Order 11246, prohibiting contractors using federal funds from discriminating in employment on the basis of race, color, religion, or national origin. While incorporating the substantive aspects of the earlier Kennedy order, it made major changes in the organizational structure of the program. Perhaps most important, contractors were required to develop affirmative action plans in order to remain eligible for federal contracts (Greenberger, 1980). Full authority was delegated to the Secretary of Labor to administer the provisions regarding nondiscrimination in employment by government contractors. Subsequently, the Secretary of Labor established the Office of Federal Contract Compliance as the operating arm of affirmative action. Johnson's original order did not refer to sex, however. Not until 1968 was "sex" added to the list of prohibited forms of discrimination in employment by federal contractors.

Beginning in 1966 and continuing through 1968, the Office of Federal Contract Compliance gradually began to exercise its enforcement power with respect to racial discrimination. The Office established procedures for hearings to determine violations and policies for the imposition of sanctions. They issued eight notices of proposed debarment, although only two proceeded to the point of decision. Decisions in these two cases—*Allen-Bradley* and *Bethlehem Steel*—provided the basis for subsequent government action in the affirmative action area.

The *Allen-Bradley* case focused on recruitment policies. In its decision the government ruled that the company had failed to take affirmative action to broaden its recruitment base, specifically with reference to the flow of minority applicants. The *Bethlehem Steel* case involved a conflict between seniority and affirmative action. The government concluded that past discrimination was perpetuated at the Sparrows Point, Maryland plant by assigning blacks to jobs and departments that had limited opportunities for advancement. It was further found that the wage pattern favored white workers. As a result of these findings, the government ordered Bethlehem Steel to make sweeping changes in its seniority system at Sparrows Point. To offset the effects of past discrimination, the order also required the company to offer blacks transfers to better jobs.

According to Jones (1976), the Nixon administration met several major problems and substantial disarray in the affirmative action area when it assumed office. One of the problems was "the addition of sex to the protected classes . . . without any comparable program having been developed to accomodate the new complaint universe of women" (Jones, 1976, p. 190).

The first affirmative action initiative of the Nixon administration was the *Philadelphia Plan* in the construction industry. This plan, subsequently defended in Congress and in the courts, made possible an articulation of the affirmative action obligation. Thus, "the use of the utilization analysis (determination of underutilization and resort to goals and timetables to insure equality of minority participation) was not possible prior to the *Philadelphia Plan* exercise" (Jones, 1976, p. 196).

The utilization analysis is the crux of Order No. 4 issued by the Department of Labor in January of 1970. This order required federal contractors to take affirmative action with respect to minorities; in December 1971 a revised order was issued that included women in the provisions as well.

It is important to note that these mandates target the *consequences* of disparate representation. In other words, the government does not have to prove intent on the part of the organization, but simply has to demonstrate that disproportionate representation of certain classes does exist. Unless a company can show that such unequal representation is a "business necessity," unlawful discrimination is said to exist.

Consent decrees have been one widely adopted means of correcting such disproportionate representation. A consent decree is a legally binding agreement between various agencies of the U.S. government and the institutions involved, often resulting from threatened litigation but in lieu of a final court proceeding. In a highly publicized case in 1973, the American Telephone and Telegraph Company signed a consent decree dealing with the employment of women. In this settlement, the company agreed to provide $15 million in restitution and back pay for several classes of female employees and to institute a $23 million promotion package for women and minorities.

On April 12, 1974, a steel industry consent decree was signed by nine major steel companies and the United Steelworkers of America, covering more than 340,000 bargaining-unit workers in 250 plants. In addition to back pay, this consent decree required complex and major revisions in the seniority system of virtually the entire industry.

With particular reference to trade and craft occupations, the steel industry consent decree required management to analyze each craft job in terms of its minority and female representation. When such representation was disproportionately low, the companies were required to establish goals for minority groups and for females. An implementing ratio of 50 percent was established for transfer into the crafts and associated apprenticeships, to be maintained until the stipulated goals were achieved. In other words, 50 percent of all new transfers into the craft occupations were to be either minority or female group members. Seniority policies were altered to facilitate these goals. First, seniority factors are now applied separately to each group for whom timetables are established. Second, rules of seniority were changed so that the worker no longer loses seniority when switching from one department to another. Thus craft positions must be bid for on a plant-wide basis, rather than being restricted within a single unit. Outside applicants are considered only when there are no qualified bidders within the plant.

During the past two decades, most states have adopted laws similar to the federal legislation, dealing both with equal pay and with equal employment opportunity. Not all gender-related employment issues are resolved (e.g., the issue of comparable worth of male- and female-dominated occupations) and there is certainly not complete equity. Yet current laws are clearly based on quite different assumptions than were the earlier protective legislation.

LEGAL RESPONSE TO SEXUAL HARASSMENT

Perhaps the most recent development in policy and litigation involving women at work concerns sexual harassment. As discussed in the previous chapter, surveys have reported substantial numbers of sexual harassment incidents in the work setting, mainly, but not exclusively, directed at women.

As described by Faley, sexual discrimination "is manifested in the workplace by the repeated assertion of an employees' sexual identity over his/her identity as a worker" (1982, p. 4). This conception of role priorities is quite different from the assumptions underlying early protective legislation. There, the sexual identity of a worker took precedence over the identity as a worker. Here, we find that protection is directed at insuring women the right of primacy of the worker, over her sexual, role. This shift in priorities represents a key aspect of recent public policy following from the Civil Rights Act.

Federal courts did not hear the first case based on complaints of sexual harassment until 1974, ten years after the enactment of the Civil Rights Act. The plaintiffs in the initial case (e.g., *Corne* v. *Bausch & Lomb, Inc.*, *Barnes* v. *Train, Miller* v. *Bank of America*) were not successful. The argument of the defense in these cases was that harassment was not gender-specific, and hence was outside of the purview of the Civil Rights Act. The courts concurred, concluding that sexual harassment was a "personal matter" (Faley, 1982, p. 6).

In the 1976 *Williams* v. *Saxbe* decision, this policy changed. The courts ruled in this case that a complainant did not have to prove that the behavior occurs only to one sex, but only that the behavior creates an "artificial barrier to employment that was placed before one gender and not the other, even though both genders were similarly situated" (quoted in Faley, 1982, p. 7). Thus if an employer effectively sets up a double standard, demanding sexual interchanges with one sex and not the other, then the policy is interpreted to be in violation of Title VII. Further loosening the restrictions in this area, the courts have not required a complainant to establish that all members of one group have been victimized. Thus a single incident of harassment can be the basis for a suit against discriminatory practices (Faley, 1982).

SUMMARY

In the past 100 years, there have been continuous changes in the policies that surround women's employment. For the first several decades of this century, policy and legislation were aimed at "protecting" women. These policies effectively put the role of woman before that of worker, positing that certain characteristics of women distinguished them from workers (or men) and that these distinctions must be preserved through law. As recently as 1948, courts ruled that there could be a "rational basis" for prohibiting some jobs to women.

Equal employment rights for women were not guaranteed for women under law until the Civil Rights Act of 1964. Since then, affirmative action policies and procedures have been developed to assure women of these rights.

Reality may not always reflect the legal standards. In spite of court rulings, women may not be hired as readily as men, they may be terminated more often, or they may be sexually harassed. Yet the legal precedents have been established, and there is some recourse if these standards are not followed. Unlike the "protective" legislation of the past, current laws are designed to expand rather than restrict women's areas of employment.

NOTE

1. For a more detailed account of legislation affecting the employment of women, the following texts are recommended: R. S. Ratner (Ed.), *Equal employment policy for women: Strategies for implementation in the United States, Canada, and Western Europe*. Philadelphia: Temple University Press, 1981; and H. H. Kay, *Text, cases and materials on sex-based discrimination* (2nd ed.). St. Paul, Minn.: West, 1981.

4

The Basic Steel Industry

Steel has long been the world's most important industrial material. Yet although the status of the steel industry is often used as a benchmark for estimates of the economy, many people know little about the industry itself—either about the manufacture of steel, the conditions within a steel mill, or the standing of the steel industry in the overall economic picture. To understand the situation of women of steel, it is necessary to describe, if only briefly, the U.S. steel industry.

THE MANUFACTURING OF STEEL

The steel industry, as defined by Crandall (1981), is a set of establishments that produce finished steel mill products and semifinished slabs, blooms, and billets from iron ore, steel scrap, or both. These terms, like the process itself, are unfamiliar to many. Basically, the constituents of steel are iron and carbon, with other chemicals added to produce different types of alloys. The varieties of steel are numerous, but a limited number of methods produce all types.

As shown in Figure 4.1, the process of steelmaking begins with the production of coke (which is coal baked in the absence of air). Coke, when combined with limestone processed in a sintering plant, and iron ore, is then transformed into iron in the blast furnaces. The iron is later refined into steel, through one of three basis processes.

Open hearth furnaces, which were the predominant method for

making steel until the late 1960s, operate much as a primitive oven, sweeping flames across a shallow hearth to provide the heat necessary to melt the charge. With the advent of the basic oxygen furnace, which requires much shorter heating times, efficiency of steelmaking has improved substantially. Computer controls typically regulate the making of steel in this method. In 1980, 60 percent of steel production was done through use of the basic oxygen furnace, far surpassing the 11 percent produced by the older open hearth method (American Iron and Steel Institute, 1982). In recent years, a third method—the electric furnace—has also become widely used, accounting for 28 percent of steel production in 1980. The advantages of this method are its ability to use a greater percentage of steel scrap and its cleaner operation, the latter a clear advantage in view of recent enforcement of pollution standards. Table 4.1 shows raw steel output by furnace type in selected recent years.

The difference between electric furnace production and integrated steel production using the open hearth or basic oxygen furnaces is illustrated in Figure 4.1. In what is termed the 'fully integrated" steel mill, necessary facilities include iron ore yards, coal yards, coke ovens, sintering plants, and blast furnaces. All of these facilities are needed to prepare the molten iron used in the open hearth or basic oxygen furnace. In contrast,

TABLE 4.1   U.S. Raw Steel Output by Furnace Type 1965, 1970, 1975, and 1981 Output

	Basic Oxygen Furnace	Open Hearth Furnace	Electric Furnace	Total
	Thousands of Net Tons			
1965	22,879	94,193	13,804	130,876
1970	63,330	48,022	20,162	131,514
1975	71,801	22,161	22,680	116,642
1981	73,231	13,452	34,145	120,828
	Percent ot Total			
1965	17.5	72.0	10.5	
1970	48.2	36.5	15.3	
1975	61.6	19.0	19.4	
1980	60.6	11.1	28.3	

Source: American Iron and Steel Institute, 1982, p. 55.

FIGURE 4.1 Steel Production Processes

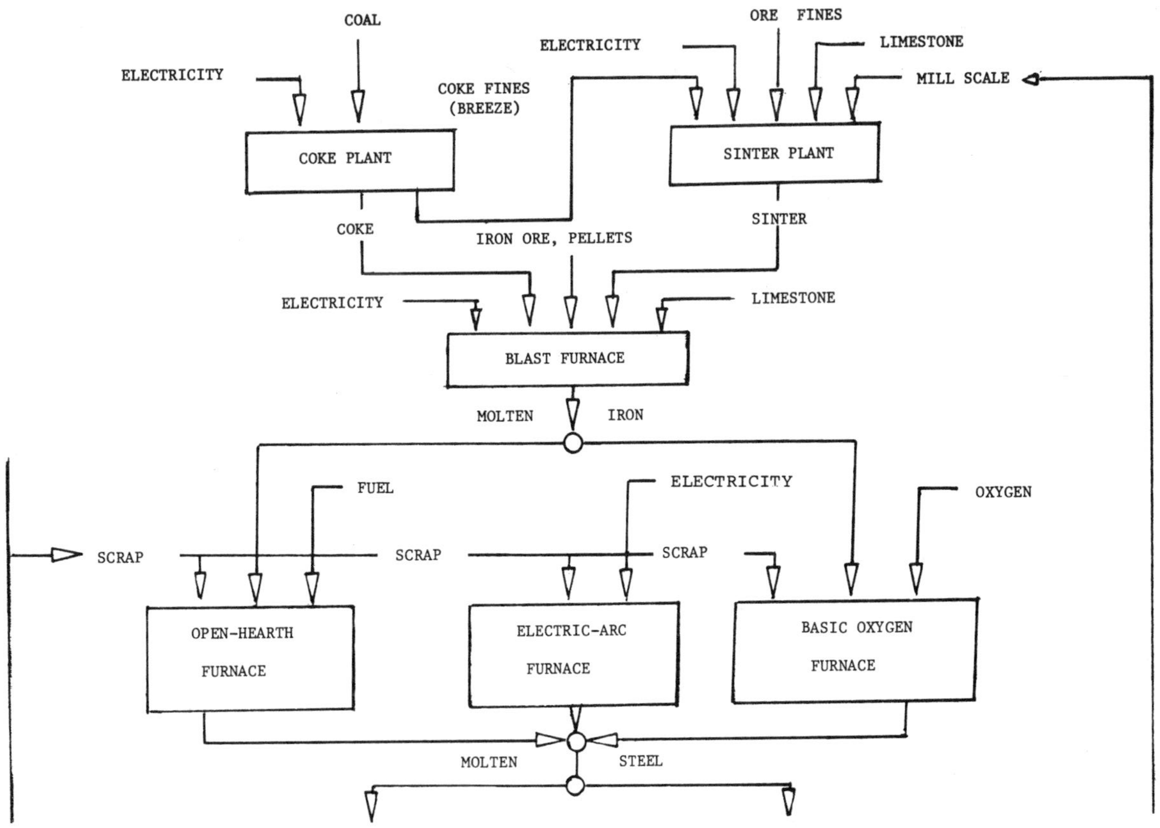

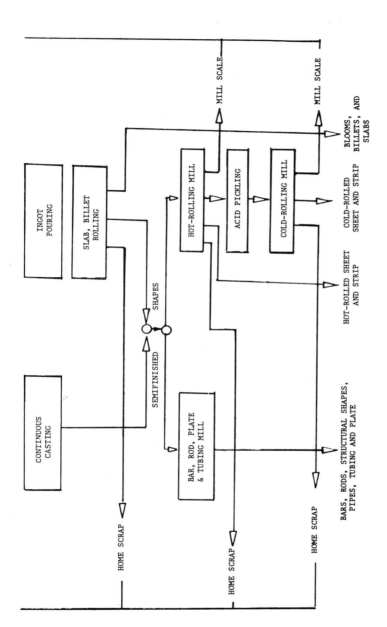

Note: A circle at a junction indicates alternatives.

Source: U.S. Council of Wage and Price Stability, 1977, p. 14.

57

only scrap and electricity are required to produce steel in an electric furnace.

From the steelmaking furnace forward, there is little difference between an electric furnace and an integrated mill. As Figure 4.1 shows, steel is either formed into ingots and then rolled, or it is cast directly into semifinished form through continuous casting. The latter process is one of the notable improvements in modern steelmaking, reducing the time required to make slabs from many hours to approximately 45 minutes.

Semifinished shapes produced by the casting process are then rolled, forged, or shaped into finished steel products. These final products fall into four major categories: (1) sheets used in automobiles, appliances, and cans; (2) plates, which are heavier than sheets and are used in shipbuilding, construction, and similar products; (3) bars, such as reinforcing rods used in construction; and (4) wire and tubular products.

Description of the process of steelmaking alone can not convey the sense of enormity that one experiences when entering the grounds of a steel mill. Often covering dozens of acres, the integrated steel mill typically provides a new experience in size and perspective. The product is big, the equipment is big, and the buildings are big, giving the first-time visitor the sense of being a shrunken Alice entering Wonderland. Travel from one department to another—for example, from the blast furnaces to the rolling mills—is best accomplished by car or bus.

In addition to the size, it is impossible to ignore the environmental conditions. These conditions, the subject of considerable controversy and legislation in recent years, may vary greatly. Although the typical image of a steel mill invokes visions of dirt, noise, and heat, these elements may or may not be part of a particular department or a particular plant. Some areas of the mill are clearly dirty—the blast furnaces and the coke ovens, for example. Other departments, at what is called the finishing end of the process, may be quite clean, particularly in the more modern steel plants. The same variation is true of the temperature conditions. In the blast furnaces, temperatures may range into the hundreds, even in winter. Yet in other areas of the mill, workers operate from air-conditioned booths, oblivious to the heat on the floor below.

Workers operating within this environment must be constantly aware of safety regulations. Hard hats are required at all times, for visitors as well as workers. In addition, workers are supplied with safety glasses, protective shoes, and gloves. The dangers of work in the steel mills characteristic of the turn of the century, described vividly by Davis (1972) and others, no longer predominate. Yet accidents still do happen, and constant precautions must be taken.

THE STATUS OF THE STEEL INDUSTRY

For many decades, steel has accounted for 90 percent or more of the total production of all metals, including both industrial and precious metals. Worldwide steel production was 781 million tons in 1981, of which 121 million tons were produced in the United States.

Steel production is the fourth largest industry in the United States, exceeded only by food, petroleum, and automative (American Iron and Steel Institute, 1980). The steel industry has provided over 4 percent of total manufacturing payrolls in the country, and value added by the industry represents about 1 percent of the gross national product.[1] Yet in recent years, the preeminence of the U.S. steel industry has been severely shaken. Profitability has become a major issue. As shown in Table 4.2, the steel industry compared favorably with other manufacturing industries in 1950 in terms of the return on equity after taxes. Yet while this ratio stayed relatively constant for other industries in the subsequent 30 years, that rate has fallen sharply for steel manufacturers.

Foreign competition has cut severely into U.S. steel company profits. Following World War II, the U.S. industry accounted for more than one-half of total world steel production, but that position has eroded steadily in subsequent years. In 1981, for example, the 121 million tons produced in the United States lagged far behind the Soviet Union's 164 million ton production, and barely ahead of Japan's 112 million tons. European

TABLE 4.2. Rate of Return on Equity After Taxes: Steel Versus all Manufacturing, 1950, 1955, 1960, 1965, 1970, 1975 and 1978 (in percent)

Year	Primary U.S. Iron and Steel Firms	All U.S. Manufacturing
1950	14.3	15.4
1955	13.5	12.6
1960	7.2	9.2
1965	9.8	13.0
1970	4.3	9.3
1975	10.9	11.6
1978	8.9	15.0

Source: Federal Trade Commission-Securities and Exchange Commission, Quarterly Financial Reports for Manufacturing Corporations (Government Printing Office, 1950) and subsequent selected quarterly issues through 1978.

Economic Community countries (primarily West Germany, France, and the United Kingdom) produced an additional 138 million tons. Together, these other nations produced 68 percent of total world steel production in 1981.

Steel imports made their first significant inroads into the domestic market in the late 1950s and early 1960s, particularly in connection with the 116-day-long steel strike of 1959. Since the mid-1960s, imports have taken between 12 percent and 19 percent of the domestic market, reaching a high of 19 percent in 1981 (American Iron and Steel Institute, 1982). All indications are that this share is continuing to rise. In many ways, U.S. steel executives failed to anticipate the potential impact of foreign competition. The steel industry in Japan, for example, has developed much more rapidly than many anticipated. The initial condescension of some U.S. executives to Japanese capability is illustrated in the comment of one executive, made in 1972. "The Japanese can't make steel," he predicted; "they're not big enough" (Almond, 1981).

For many reasons, the U.S. steel industry currently faces severe productivity and profitability problems. In 1977–78, the net income for the industry fell to virtually zero, and plant closings and production cutbacks became rampant. A recent Brookings Institution study (Crandall, 1981) summarizes the economic situation of the basic steel industry:

> The events of 1977–78 were not unique. The U.S. steel industry has faced recurrent crises since the late 1950s. Imports began to surge in 1959 when steelmakers faced a long strike; throughout the 1960s they struggled with sluggish growth, rising imports, low profits, and repeated confrontations with government on pricing policies. . . .
>
> Despite protectionism during the 1969–1974 period, the industry did not rebound from the doldrums of the 1960s. Although in 1974 strong demand and the abandonment of price controls combined to produce a profitable year, the 1976 recession plunged the industry back into a depressed state—a condition from which it has not recovered. The slow growth of the 1960s has not been replaced by an actual reduction of total industry capacity. Environmental costs have risen sharply. Labor costs have been rising at a precipitous rate. After two major bouts of trade protection, the industry appears to be in a more precarious position than ever. (p. 3)

Events of 1981 and 1982 have borne out Crandall's gloomy prognosis. By late 1982, steel production as a percentage of capacity had fallen below 40 percent, its lowest level since the Depression. Almost 50 percent of the work force had been laid off. Industry observers and executives are predicting a permanent reduction in U.S. steel capacity of 10 percent within three years and 20 percent by 1990 (*Business Week*, May 1982).

Many reasons have been offered for this decline in the industry. It is clear that U.S. steel plants are much older and less efficient than those of many of the foreign competitors. In the United States, for example, only one major fully integrated plant has been built in the past 20 years, and technological improvements in equipment are lagging far behind those of other countries, most notably Japan. When such improvements are made, U.S. companies sometimes even find it necessary to hire Japanese consultants to supervise the installation of new equipment.

A number of critics have pointed to the failure of the U.S. steel industry to invest adequately in research and development, choosing instead to focus on shorter-term profits. According to some estimates, the U.S. steel industry spends less than 1 percent of its revenues on research and development. Within the United States, only lumber and textiles devote a smaller percentage to research (Almond, 1981). This failure to reinvest profits in the industry itself was recently illustrated by U.S. Steel Corporation's merger with Marathon Oil Company. U.S. Steel, the nation's largest steel producer, consumated a $6.4 billion merger in late 1981, a move widely seen as having important negative consequences for the domestic steel industry because it diverted capital needed for modernization to other uses. Evaluating this move, the editors of *Business Week* magazine voiced the opinions of many, stating that "the U.S. cannot let foreign producers simply move in and take over its steel industry. Yet it cannot meet foreign competition just by erecting high tariff walls to protect the domestic industry from its own shortcomings . . . the only remedy is substantial investment in modernization. The $6 billion U.S. Steel (Corporation) is spending on Marathon should go into that effort" (*Business Week*, December 1981, p. 144).

Other factors have also been cited in attempts to explain the unhealthy state of the U.S. steel industry. The cost of government regulation is one such factor. The steel industry is subject to three principal kinds of regulation: environmental regulation, occupational health and safety programs, and equal employment opportunity and affirmative action programs.

The production of steel requires a substantial number of dirty and/or dangerous activities, as noted earlier. Many of the processes generate air- and water-borne pollutants, which are potentially harmful to both workers and to residents living near the steel mills. Further, the heat, smoke, and heavy equipment associated with steelmaking create significant worker safety problems. To ameliorate the impact of the environmental, and health and safety problems, the industry has been required to institute a variety of pollution control devices and equipment. It should be noted that in many cases, required standards are not as strict as they are in some other countries, most notably Japan. Nonetheless the cost of installing such equipment in facilities not originally designed for such additions is considerable.

According to a study by the Environmental Protection Agency (Temple, Barber, and Sloane, 1977), the average cost of steel products will be increased by 4.6 percent by 1983 due to required pollution outlays. Using American Iron and Steel Institute data, Crandall (1981) estimates that total environmental outlays may eventually rise to 5.5 percent of product prices. Yet he concludes that environmental costs "could hardly be said to be a major cause of the industry's current problems" (1981, p. 39).

Costs of the other two forms of regulations—safety and affirmative action—appear to be less substantial. According to the steel industry's own estimates, occupational health and safety regulation costs are only about one-sixth of the environmental costs (American Iron and Steel Institute, 1980). Thus, the combined costs of environmental and health and safety programs should add no more than about 6.4 percent to industry costs by 1983. Interestingly, neither the Crandall (1981) nor the American Iron and Steel Institute (1980) studies make reference to any actual or possible costs of equal employment opportunity or affirmative action programs. It seems plausible to infer that neither set of investigators believed that these costs were very great. Alternatively, it is possible that there is simply no basis for estimating such costs.

The third major target for analysis of the current state of the steel industry is the wage scale of the employees. To understand the impact of this factor, it is necessary to look at the overall picture of steel industry employment.

EMPLOYMENT IN THE STEEL INDUSTRY

American steel companies employed 391,000 workers in 1981 (American Iron and Steel Institute, 1982). The companies paid wages and salaries of $11.9 billion to the workers. Yet because of increasing mechanization and the absence of industry growth, steel industry employment has been falling for several decades. As Table 4.3 shows, employees engaged in steel production and marketing in the basic steel industry fell from nearly 600,000 in 1965 to less than 400,000 in 1981, a decline of 33 percent. During the same period, the number of workers receiving wages—basically the union workers, as opposed to the salaried management personnel—declined from over 400,000 to less than 300,000, a drop of nearly 38 percent. Because of the modest reduction in the length of the average workweek in the industry between 1965 and 1981, total hours worked declined even more than the numbers employed.

The steel industry can be described as a labor-intensive industry. The

TABLE 4.3. Employment and Hours Worked in the Iron and Steel Industry (only those employees engaged in production and sale of iron and steel products)

	Employees Receiving Wages		Employees Receiving Salaries		All Employees	
	Average No. of Employees	Average Hours Worked per Week	Average No. of Employees	Average Hours Worked per Week	Average No. of Employees	Average Hours Worked per Week
1965	458,539	37.7	125,312	39.3	583,851	38.0
1970	403,115	36.7	128,081	38.7	531,196	37.2
1975	339,945	35.1	177,217	38.3	457,162	35.9
1981	286,219	36.4	104,695	38.5	390,914	36.9

Source: American Iron and Steel Institute, 1982, p. 21.

ratio of labor payments to total value added has remained high even in prosperous years, in comparison with all manufacturing industries. Between 1972 and 1976, U.S. manufacturing industries paid an average of 51 percent value added to workers in the form of wages and benefits. For the same period, the steel industry paid labor an average of 64 percent of its value added, even though 1973 and 1974 were boom years for steel (Crandall, 1981). By this measure, the steel industry is even more labor intensive than the apparel and electronics industries, which averaged 58 percent and 57 percent, respectively, during the same period.

Wages in the U.S. steel industry have always been high, relative to wages in other industries. From 1957 to 1973, hourly earnings for workers in the steel industry ranged from 26 percent to 42 percent above hourly earnings of workers in all manufacturing (see Table 4.4 for a detailed presentation). Since 1974, steel wages have risen particularly rapidly in comparison with the U.S. average for manufacturing wages. In dollar figures, the 1981 average steel worker employment cost per hour was $20.16, including fringe benefits and pay for time not worked (American Iron and Steel Institute, 1982).

Not only are wages of U.S. steel workers high relative to other domestic industries, but they are high in comparison to foreign workers as well. In an interesting analysis, Crandall (1981) shows that the ratio of steel industry wages to all manufacturing wages is much higher in the United States than in Japan and Germany, two principal competitors. A similar discrepancy exists in the wages within the automobile industry, but not in chemicals,

TABLE 4.4. Average Hourly Earnings in the U.S. Steel
Industry and in All U.S. Manufacturing 1957–81

	Steel Industry	*Manufacturing*	*Ratio of Steel to Manufacturing*
1957	$2.78	2.04	1.34
1958	2.91	2.10	1.39
1959	3.10	2.19	1.42
1960	3.08	2.26	1.36
1961	3.20	2.32	1.38
1962	3.29	2.39	1.38
1963	3.36	2.45	1.37
1964	3.41	2.53	1.35
1965	3.46	2.61	1.33
1966	3.58	2.71	1.32
1967	3.62	2.82	1.28
1968	3.82	3.01	1.27
1969	4.09	3.19	1.28
1970	4.22	3.35	1.26
1971	4.57	3.57	1.28
1972	5.17	3.82	1.35
1973	5.61	4.09	1.37
1974	6.41	4.42	1.45
1975	7.12	4.83	1.47
1976	7.79	5.22	1.49
1977	8.59	5.68	1.51
1978	9.70	6.17	1.57
1979	10.77		
1980	11.84		
1981	13.11		

Source: American Iron and Steel Institute, 1982; and Crandall, 1981.

machinery, paper, or electronics and electrical equipment. Given the importance of labor payments in value added in steel and automobiles, and the high relative U.S. wage, Crandall observes that it is not surprising that U.S. steel and automobile industries have great difficulty competing with imports.

The sharp rise in steel industry wages since 1974 is due primarily to the adoption of the pioneering Experimental Negotiating Agreement (ENA) between 11 large integrated steel firms and the United Steelworkers of America in 1973. Under the ENA, workers agreed not to strike in return for substantial wage concessions.

The impetus for the ENA was the "boom-or-bust" cycle that had developed in the industry after 1959. In 1959, the 116-day strike by unions created apprehension on the part of steel users. Wary of similar strike possibilities in the future, users and steel mills themselves began stockpiling large amounts of steel to protect themselves should such strikes occur. Many users also began looking to foreign producers to provide alternate sources of steel. Yet no strikes occurred during the 1962–63, 1965, and 1968 negotiations. Consequently, industry production fell and number of employees decreased due to the large inventories built up prior to the strike deadlines.

To overcome this unprofitable cycle, the industry decided that there was a need to guarantee that there would be no industry-wide strikes in the future. Thus the ENA, which established an agreement between union and management that no national strike would take place. As a result, stockpiling subsided and the level of production and employment remained more stable.

In retrospect, the price paid for no strikes seems high. Workers were given a 3 percent annual wage increase, a liberalized cost-of-living escalator clause, and a $150 bonus. Given the small productivity growth after 1973, this agreement was clearly expensive. Further, the ENA put a floor under the 1974, 1977, and 1980 negotiations that assured similar expensive settlements in each of these years.

In summary, the U.S. steel industry rapidly became the best-paying blue-collar job in the country. Yet the appeal of such an employment site for the worker has clearly been tempered in recent years by the drastic decline in productivity and resultant layoffs approaching 35 percent. For the industry as a whole, the message of the tea leaves is not favorable. Whether one lays the responsibility on high wages, costs of government regulation, or lack of foresight by management, it is clear that the immediate future is much less promising than the past.

NOTE

1. Value added is computed by deducting total raw material costs of the steel produced by the industry from total dollar revenues received by the industry from sales of steel. Alternatively, value added included industry labor costs, indirect costs and profit.

5

Studying
Women of Steel

A general understanding of the steel industry provides the context for our study of women in two particular steel mills. We approached these steel plants with some specific questions concerning women (and men) of steel. Those specific objectives will be outlined first. Then we will describe the ways in which we attempted to answer the questions, and finally, we will describe the women themselves, as well as their male coworkers and the supervisors who oversee them.

OBJECTIVES OF THE RESEARCH

At the most general level, we wanted to find out everything we could about the situation for women in the steel mills. As most researchers know, however, such global interests need to be focused. Even a single steel plant is a tremendous place, employing as many as 20,000 or 30,000 workers, covering hundreds of acres of land, and going back in history for perhaps 50 to 75 years. Given this scope of time, place, and numbers, an investigator must be selective, deciding which questions are most important and which methods will be most likely to yield answers to those questions.

Moving from our general concern with women in the steel mills and the effects of affirmative action consent decrees, we formulated several specific questions to be pursued in detail.

1. *Have the consent decrees had a noticeable effect on the hiring patterns for*

more responsibility and that provide a path to more advanced positions. Supervisors of training (the journeymen in the craft occupations) may not provide women with the instruction necessary to learn a new job or skill. Supervisors and male workers alike may provide an unfavorable climate for women. Negative attitudes may be conveyed through words and gestures, by statements about the incompatibility of women and steel mills, or by professed beliefs in the home as women's proper place. More directly, male coworkers may directly express antagonism, engage in unusual hazing procedures, or make women the brunt of foul jokes and unwarranted pranks. Even more seriously, sexual harassment can be a critical issue.

The possible existence of such barriers—either internal or external—needs to be documented in order to understand how blue-collar women function in traditionally male settings.

4. *Has the hiring of women affected the ability of the industry to meet other affirmative action goals?* As we have noted, much of the impetus for hiring women in the steel mills followed the signing of consent decrees with the government, assuring that a certain percentage of women would be hired. Yet before women were targeted by government policy, other groups had been the focus of concern, specifically black and other minority males. From a policy perspective, it is worth considering how well these two sets of goals fit together. Has the new emphasis on hiring women had any negative effects on previous efforts to hire more minority men?

Certainly government policy makers did not tell employers to hire and promote women instead of minority males. Indeed, this idea would be abhorrent to those responsible for equal employment opportunity and affirmative action programs. On the other hand, employers have only a certain number of new job openings and a limited number of promotion opportunities. A particular opening can be filled by only one person, be that person black, Hispanic, or white, man or woman. Furthermore, if male workers perceive such displacements and preferential treatments, then additional negative barriers may confront the female worker.

5. *How do the women themselves view their jobs as blue-collar steel workers?* As we noted in Chapter 2, there is considerable disagreement as to what kinds of jobs women want and what characteristics they want those jobs to have. Blue-collar work, particularly in the steel industry, has not been a traditional choice for women. What kinds of women are now in the steel industry, taking advantage of newly created opportunites? Knowing more about the likes and dislikes, hopes and misgivings of this selected group of women can furnish important insights into women workers as a whole.

These were the general objectives of our research inquiry. To answer these questions, we developed a number of methods that will be described in the next section. In attempting to answer these questions, we had a twofold purpose. First, we wanted to provide information for those who are concerned about blue-collar workers, particularly those in the steel industry. For academicians and laypersons alike, such information can be very useful. A second purpose was more ambitious. In providing some basic information, we hoped to be able to suggest new options as well. Knowing what works and where some of the problems are, both management and policymakers should be able to benefit. Thus our aims are both descriptive and prescriptive—in describing the present situation we hope to provide some guidelines for future action.

METHODS OF RESEARCH

This investigation focused on two selected steel mills, chosen for a variety of reasons. Concerns that the findings not be unique to a particular setting dictated that we select more than one plant, while limits of time and money required that the number of study plants be manageable. Another critical factor in selection was gaining the cooperation of the management of the steel plants, allowing us to acquire records, interview workers and supervisors, and obtain necessary background information. Such a commitment is not always easily gained. First, there are the obvious cost factors involved for the company; considerable person-hours are being contributed to a project that may or may not yield any concrete benefits for the company. A second concern to many firms in recent years is the possibility of negative consequences when a study concerns the role of women or minorities in the work force. Given the age of litigation in which we live, evidence of negative treatment of women, for example, could provide the grounds for suits against a company. Thus many companies prefer to restrict exploration of minority or female status to an "in-house" basis, so that results of studies can be kept out of the public domain.

We initially contacted four companies. Two of these firms agreed to cooperate fully, sharing records, providing company time and facilities for interviews, and meeting with us from time to time to explore related issues. In addition, each of these firms arranged a tour of the plant for our research team, so that we could become familiar at first hand with the operation of a modern steel plant. Management of the two other companies declined to participate in the study.

The two plants in the study employed a combined total of approximately 34,000 workers in 1979; of this total, 4168 workers were women. Both of the study mills are profitable, relatively modern plants, and both had shown stable to rising employment during the five years prior to the study. In addition, both plants are considered by observers within and outside the industry to be well-managed plants. Thus our study plants are not completely typical of the domestic steel industry. They represent the healthiest segment of that industry, they are in no apparent danger of closing, and their rising employment has allowed the increased hiring of women. This last point is critical. If a plant did not have an expanding labor force, then neither good intentions nor consent decrees could have much impact on female employment.

Once the study plants were selected, our task was straightforward, if not particularly easy—to attempt to answer the questions that we posed in approaching the mills. We used four general approaches to answer these questions: (1) informal interviews with personnel and training executives; (2) examination of company employment records; (3) interviews with a sample of supervisors; and (4) interviews with samples of male and female workers.

Informal Interviews

An initial requirement for us, as investigators, was to become totally familiar to the operation of the steel mills, with hiring and training practices, and with the beliefs and feelings that surround the issue of women blue-collar workers. Such general information not only allowed us to gain an overall familiarity with the environment, but it also provided information needed to construct interview forms.

Discussion with personnel managers at each firm made it obvious that the issue of hiring women was not one free of passion. Many of the people with whom we talked had strong opinions on the subject, and stories of a particular woman who was doing well (or, more often, poorly) were commonplace. It also became clear that many of these opinions were based on single incidents or secondhand reports. In very few instances had the companies collected any data that would support or refute the beliefs that were held.

Both companies used some type of outside agency to assist in the recruitment and/or training of workers, particularly female and minority group members. Accordingly, we visited these agencies as well, observing their operations and conducting lengthy interviews with the staff members at each agency. These discussions, fortified by a "hard-hat" tour of each plant, provided essential material for further exploration.

Company Records

Most companies keep extensive records of the work force, including figures for hiring, termination, and promotion. In the case of women and minorities, additional records are mandated by the federal government. In particular, companies employing more than a specified number of people must submit an "EEO" form to the government each quarter, providing an occupational breakdown of employment by sex and ethnicity. These records proved to be invaluable, and we were able to obtain records for the period from June 1973 to June 1979 at both plants. At one of the plants, records for an earlier period (June 1965 to June 1972) and for a later period (June 1980) were also made available.

As is often the case when investigators rely on archival records collected by an organization for some purpose other than the researcher's needs, many of the records that we had hoped to find or obtain were not available. Specifically, we could not get reliable information on recruitment, training, or employment costs. Similarly, no useful data were available on performance or productivity. (Gross measures of productivity were of course maintained, but these could not be broken down by worker or work group.) Records of specific daily or monthly job assignments were not kept in a usable form, nor were regular records of absenteeism and grievances available. In some cases, this information simply had not been collected in any systematic fashion. In other cases, although certain records might have been retrieved, the cost of doing so was very high from the company's viewpoint, and just justifiable in their overall operation. In still other cases, concerns for the confidentiality of workers records precluded obtaining some data that might have been useful.

In summary, the basic employment data provide an important foundation for the investigation. For many issues of concern, however, the absence of objective measures forced a reliance on interview data, obtained from the workers and supervisors themselves.

Interviews

After discussions with company officials, we decided to concentrate the interviews in four departments at each plant. There were several reasons for this decision. First, it was important to have as much comparability between the two plants as possible, and designating similar departments within each plant increased the comparability. Second, it seemed possible that women might be more successful in some departments than in others. Thus we purposely chose two departments that company officials characterized as undesirable from the standpoint of physical demands, heat, dust, and cleanliness. These two departments were the coke ovens and the blast furnaces. Two other departments were selected to represent the most desirable and least difficult locations—the plate mill and the hot mill, both at the finishing end of the steelmaking process.

Within each department, we interviewed a sample of supervisors and workers. Approximately 12 supervisors were selected from each department. These supervisors were chosen to represent all three levels of supervision (superintendent, general foremen, and turn foremen), as well as the three major divisions (production, mechanical, and electrical).

Between 25 and 30 workers, representing an approximately equal number of men and women, were interviewed from each of these same departments. In most cases, we interviewed a majority of the women in a department who were available at the time of our interviews. Male workers were selected so that approximately 80 percent matched the women in terms of seniority; the remaining 20 percent were older and had been with the company longer. Because of our emphasis on craft workers, we interviewed all women in each department who were in craft occupations; an approximately equal number of the men were in crafts as well. Within these limits, workers were scheduled in terms of their availability and their willingness to participate in the study. (To our knowledge, almost no workers refused to participate). All respondents, both supervisors and workers, signed an informed consent prior to the beginning of the interview.

The interview forms themselves were developed over a period of months and were subject to considerable revision along the way. Discussions with company personnel and with steelworkers supplemented our own background and objectives to formulate an initial version of the questionnaires. Supervisor interviews were then pretested with a group of supervisors from the personnel department at one company. Worker interviews were pretested with a small group of steelworkers from another company. Based on these initial results, we made a number of changes in each interview schedule. We had agreed in advance to obtain company approval for the questionnaires themselves, and this agreement led to some additional changes. For example, both companies insisted that specific questions concerning sexual harassment be deleted from the form. Some questions dealing with union activities and support were also ruled out. In other instances, the companies asked us to add questions targeting specific areas of concern, such as craft examination procedures.

After this rather lengthy period of construction, pretesting, compromise, and approval, two interview schedules were finalized. (These interviews are printed in the Appendix).

THE RESPONDENTS:
THE WOMEN AND MEN OF STEEL

In total, we interviewed 103 women workers, 125 men workers, and 104 supervisors in the two plants combined. Although there is really no prototypical male or female steelworker, nor any "average" supervisor, descriptions of some general patterns and trends provides some perspective.

The Women

The 103 women that were interviewed represented a mix of ethnic groups and family backgrounds. Nearly half (N=53) of the women were white, more than a third (N=38) were black, and the remainder (N=12) were Hispanic. In age, the women ranged from 20 to 56, with an average age of 29.3. Most of the women (84.5 percent) had completed high school, and some had considerably more education. Two of the women, for example, had done some college postgraduate work.

The majority of these women (61 percent) were the sole wage earner in their family, a surprisingly high figure and one clearly in contradiction with the sometimes-voiced belief that women usually work merely for "pin money." Furthermore, most of the women were not supporting only themselves: two-thirds of the women had children. Although the number of children ranged from none to seven, the typical pattern was for a woman to have two children, both of whom were six years of age or older.

Most of the women steelworkers (66 percent) had mothers who had worked as well, although only six had mothers who had worked in the steel mills. More typically, the mothers of these women were employed in service industries or in retail and trade occupations, doing fairly traditional female work, such as clerical, service, or laboring jobs. The fathers of the women held a wide variety of jobs, with many employed in blue-collar fields. Thirty-four percent of their fathers had worked in the steel mills, and 27 percent had done skilled craft work. It is also noteworthy that 77 percent of the women interviewed had some relatives who currently worked in the steel mills, thus suggesting that for many of these women the steel mills were not a totally unknown environment.

Although the mills might not have been totally foreign, few of the women (8 percent) had ever worked in a steel mill before their present job. Some women had had previous experience in labor (16 percent) or semiskilled operative jobs (13 percent); a few (1.2 percent) had done craft work. For the majority, however, the work at the steel mill was apparently a rather marked shift from their previous employment. The typical pre-mill job was office and clerical (19.5 percent) or service work (19.5 percent), and the typical setting was in retail and sales (23.7 percent) or in service companies (19.4 percent). Thus it should be emphasized that the steel industry was a new experience for most of these women; neither had they worked in the similar environments of other durable and heavy industries, nor had they done jobs that required the same kinds of physical and technical skills.

As would be expected, given the recency of the rise in female employment in the steel industry, the majority of women had not been in the mills very long. On the average, the women that we interviewed had been with their company for only two years. There was some variation, of course. The range of tenure in the company was from less than one year to 14 years.

At the time of the interviews, the women were distributed across a wide range of jobs within the mills, similar to but not identical with the distribution of males (see Table 5.1). Approximately 27 percent of the women we interviewed were in the craft occupations—either millwright, vocational mechanic, or motor inspector. This group of craft workers will be considered in more detail in Chapter 9. For the moment, we should simply note that this proportion of women in crafts is *not* representative of the mills. Overall, the number of female craft workers in the two study plants in 1979 was 197, representing approximately 10 percent of the women workers and only 2 percent of the total number of craft workers. Because of our particular interest in the craft occupations, reflecting the emphasis placed on apprenticeship and craft work in the consent decree, we tried to interview every female craft worker in the selected departments.

Nearly a third of the women in the sample (and in a proportion similar to the men) were basic laborers, the principal entry-level job within the steel mills. More notable, however, is the fact that more than 20 percent of the women in the sample had been assigned to janitorial jobs. This high proportion of women assigned to a stereotypically female job is certainly cause for further exploration. In later chapters, we will describe some of the differences in attitudes and performance requirements between the

TABLE 5.1. Job Classification of Male and Female Workers

Job Title	Males		Females	
	N	%	N	%
Millwright/vocational mechanic	33	26.4	14	13.6
Motor inspector	10	8.0	14	13.6
Clerical	0	—	3	2.9
Mobile equipment operator	8	6.4	1	1.0
Janitor	5	4.0	22	21.4
Checker/stocker	9	7.2	7	6.8
Machine operator	13	10.4	9	8.7
Labor	45	36.0	32	31.1
Other	2	1.6	1	1.0

janitorial women and women who are engaged in more traditionally male jobs. In background, too, these women are somewhat different from the "typical" female steelworker. A high proportion of the women are Hispanic (32 percent) and considerably fewer are white (32 percent, compared to 57 percent of the women in other job classifications). Compared to the other "women of steel," women holding janitorial jobs tend to be older—a median age of 37 for the janitors versus 27 for women who held other jobs. Janitorial women were also more likely to have dependents than were the other women, and they were somewhat less likely to have worked in another steel mill (5 percent versus 9 percent). They were also less likely to have worked in a durable or nondurable industry prior to their present job, suggesting a greater similarity of work setting for the women who are not in janitorial jobs. In similar fashion, the mothers of the female janitors were less likely to have held labor jobs and more likely to have done some type of professional or semiprofessional work.

In summary, we suspect that the particular subsample of women holding janitorial jobs—traditionally female jobs in a traditionally male setting—were not randomly assigned. The similarities among them and the differences between them and the other women workers would support the idea that self-selection played at least some part in their positions. Discriminatory assignment may also occur, as supervisors act on certain stereotypes concerning women, and ethnicity, and job suitability. We will explore these possibilities further in Chapter 8.

The Men

The 125 men that were interviewed also came from a variety of ethnic backgrounds, although somewhat less diverse than the women. More than two-thirds of the men ($N = 86$) were white, and only 20 percent ($N = 25$) were black; the remaining men were Hispanic ($N = 12$) or of some other ethnic background ($N = 2$). In age, the men in the sample were somewhat younger than the women overall, but not much different from the nonjanitorial women, averaging 25.9 years with a range from 19 to 62. Such an age distribution is not, however, representative of the population of male steel workers. Rather it reflects sampling choices that we made initially, attempting to equate seniority among men and women workers so that experience and age would not confound any observed differences between the two groups. Thus although our sample of women is representative of the female steelworker, the sample of men is roughly equivalent to women in tenure but not representative of the overall male population. As suggested by the reported age range, however, we did interview some older men so that differences as a function of age and experience could be explored.

As was true of the women, the majority of men (86 percent) had completed high school and some had one or more years of college. Only two had completed college and none had done postgraduate work. Sixty-nine percent of the men reported being the sole wage earner in their family; the others, presumably, had wives who also worked. On the average, the men had two children; the range for number of children was from zero to seven. In general, the men in the sample had younger children than did the women: 64 percent of the men had children under six years of age compared to 45 percent of the women. This difference is probably the result of at least two factors. First, the women in the sample were on the average 3.5 years older and hence would be more likely to have older children. Second, to the extent that the woman is the sole supporter or the principal caretaker of her family, she may be more likely to avoid full-time work with inflexible shifts until the children are old enough to be in school.

Significantly[2] fewer men (48 percent) had mothers who had worked, and the jobs that their mothers held tended to be more traditional. For the most part, their mothers had worked in retail or private service jobs (including hospitals, private homes, and hotels) and often had done clerical work. Only one man had a mother who had worked in the steel mills. The fathers of these men, in contrast, were more likely to have had similar jobs. Thirty-four percent of the fathers had worked in steel mills, 23 percent had been skilled craftworkers, and 31 percent had been semiskilled operatives. As was true of the women, the majority of men (79 percent) had relatives who also worked in a steel mill.

Most of the men, like the women, had worked elsewhere before coming to the steel mills, although for 10 percent of the men, the steel plant was their first job. Significantly more of the men than the women had previously worked in another steel mill prior to their present job. Even if not experienced in steel mills per se, many of the men had had similar work experience: 29.5 percent had held labor jobs, 21.9 percent had been semiskilled operatives, and 20 percent had worked as craftsmen in their previous job.

The modal length of time that the men had been in the steel mill was two years, paralleling the women and reflecting our attempt to balance the sample. The range of years with the company was greater for men, however, going from less than one year to 30 years. (Consequently, the mean tenure for men was significantly greater than that for women.)

The men were also distributed across a wide range of jobs within the mills (see Table 5.1), and approximately one-third of them were in craft occupations. In this and other respects, they resembled the women in the sample with the notable exception of janitorial jobs, to which only five men were assigned. No men in our sample had clerical jobs (compared to three of the women); more men than women were mobile equipment operators. In other respects, the samples were relatively comparable.

The Supervisors

The 104 supervisors who were interviewed at the two plants represented three distinct levels of supervision (see Table 5.2). Fifteen of the men were superintendents or assistant superintendents of their departments—the top level of management within a department. Another 24 supervisors represented a middle level of management: general foremen of production, mechanical, or electrical divisions, who reported to the superintendent and who had a number of lower-level supervisors responsible to them. At the first level of supervision, we interviewed 65 turn foremen who were responsible for production, mechanical, or electrical work crews. Two of these lowest level supervisors were women, the only women represented in the supervisor sample. Ethnically, this sample of supervisors was also unevenly distributed: 4 were Hispanic, 13 black, and 87 white.

Supervisors were, on the average, 42 years old, although the range was considerable, varying from 25 to 65. As would be expected, age was associated with level of supervision. The average age of upper-level supervisors (superintendents, assistant superintendents, and general foremen) was 47 years, while turn foremen averaged 39 years of age. The educational level of supervisors varied considerably, and probably reflects policies on hiring and promotion within the steel industry. One-third of the supervisors had completed their education at the high school level; another third held college degrees. The range was broad, with one supervisor having only completed sixth grade while eight had a master's degree. In general, upper-level supervisors had a college degree, while turn foremen were more apt to have only a high school diploma.

The typical supervisor had been with the company for nearly 18 years, although again the range was considerable, varying from 1 to 42 years. Time in the particular department was less, averaging 11 years, and time in

TABLE 5.2. Supervisor Sample: Distribution by Level of Supervision

	Company A	Company B
Superintendents and assistant sup.	10	5
General foremen	12	12
Turn foremen	32	33
Total	54	50

the present supervisory position averaged slightly less than 6 years. This mean figure is influenced by the fact that a couple of the supervisors had held their position for more than 20 years. A more representative figure in this case is the median 4.4 years in the current position.

Although their numbers are obviously too small to allow generalization, the two women who held supervisory positions should be described more fully. Both of the women were white and both were in their late twenties. Both also had some college education, a year and a half in one case and a B.S. in electrical engineering in the other. Both were employed at the one company in our sample that had begun hiring women earlier and that currently has a larger proportion of women in the work force.

SUMMARY

These then are the people that we interviewed, the questions that we posed, and the ways that we approached our questions. Our sample is not necessarily representative of all workers. Rather, it is specifically a case study, focused on the blue-collar woman in the steel industry at two selected sites. Comparisons with other samples is difficult, given the relative lack of research on blue-collar women. Certainly the women in our sample are paid better than many of their blue-collar sisters, benefitting from the high wages that the steelworkers' union has negotiated. The women in our sample are also younger than many blue-collar workers, but probably not significantly younger than women now working in traditionally male industries. In Walshok's (1981) study of female craft workers, for example, 77 percent of the women were 30 years of age or younger. In terms of ethnic distribution, our sample had a higher percentage of both black and Hispanic women than do national figures on working women. In fact, minorities were better represented among the women in our sample than among the men.

In short, the women of steel are not wholly representative of working women or of workers in general. Yet we believe that this sample is representative of women working in this kind of industry at this period of time. By knowing more about these women, we may gain a better understanding of the future for women in blue-collar settings.

NOTES

1. In most cases, manufacturing industries have not used measures of strength as a basis for hiring decisions, in large part because the necessary data were not available. In recent years, however, there has been considerable interest in assessing the physical requirements of jobs

(see, for example, E.A. Fleishman & J.C. Hogan, *A taxonomic method for assessing the physical requirements of jobs: The physical abilities analysis approach*. Advanced Research Resources Organization, Washington, D.C., June 1978). Arnold et al. (1982), on the basis of their research at Armco Steel, recommend using arm dynamometer measures as a criterion for selection of hourly steelworkers.

2. For the sake of readability, we will not report results of statistical analyses in the text. However, the reader can assume that the use of the word "significant" means that findings were statistically significant at the .05 level or beyond.

6

Female Employment in
the Steel Industry:
Patterns and Policies

One of the goals of this research, as noted in the previous chapter, was to determine whether the consent decree had any noticeable effect on female employment in the steel industry, and in particular, in the two plants selected for study. Before looking at patterns in these two plants more closely, however, it is useful to look at the broader picture of female employment in the steel industry and in durable manufacturing generally. It will also be instructive, having considered the trends in female employment, to consider the possible effects of increased female hiring on other segments of the labor force.

FEMALE EMPLOYMENT
IN THE STEEL INDUSTRY

In 1965, women held 35 percent of all jobs in the United States; by 1980 women's share of all jobs had risen to 42 percent (Bureau of Labor Statistics, *Employment and Unemployment*, 1981). As noted in earlier chapters, the jobs that women hold do not represent a random sample of all jobs in the economy. Rather, women tend to be concentrated in a relatively small number of jobs, and are underrepresented in many fields traditionally the province of men. As Table 6.1 shows, women's share of all manufacturing jobs has been less than their share of total jobs throughout the years since 1965, yet this share has also risen. In durable manufacturing, women held 18 percent of all jobs in 1965. This figure had increased to 25 percent by

TABLE 6.1. Total Employees and Women Employees in Manufacturing, Durable Manufacturing, and Primary Metal or Steel Industry Payrolls

| | Manufacturing | | | Durable Manufacturing | | | Primary Metals (Steel: 1977–80) | | |
| | Employment | | | Employment | | | Employment | | |
	Total	Women	% Women	Total	Women	% Women	Total	Women	% Women
1965	18,062	4768	26.4%	10,406	1889	18.2%	1301	77	5.9%
1966	19,214	5214	27.1	11,284	2182	19.3	1351	85	6.3
1967	19,447	5353	27.5	11,439	2277	19.9	1332	88	6.6
1968	19,781	5490	27.8	11,626	2338	20.1	1316	90	6.8
1969	20,167	5667	28.1	11,895	2446	20.6	1361	96	7.0
1970	19,349	5436	28.1	11,195	2278	20.3	1316	93	7.1
1971	18,572	5191	28.0	10,597	2111	19.9	1229	88	7.2
1972	19,090	5411	28.3	11,006	2259	20.5	1240	89	7.2
1973	20,068	5803	28.6	11,839	2547	21.5	1324	100	7.6
1974	20,046	5819	29.0	11,895	2606	21.9	1344	104	7.7
1975	18,347	5259	28.7	10,679	2274	21.3	1180	92	7.8
1976	18,956	5590	29.5	11,026	2446	22.2	1190	101	8.5
1977	19,554	5816	29.7	11,480	2612	22.8	1203	108	9.0
1977	20,637	6150	29.8	12,274	2872	23.4	510	38	7.5
1978	21,497	6554	30.5	12,821	3101	24.2	467	36	7.7
1979	22,137	6834	30.9	13,450	3369	25.1	501	45	9.0
1980	21,593	6786	31.4	12,993	3294	25.4	437	31	7.1

Sources: 1965–77 data are from U.S. Department of Labor, *Handbook of Labor Statistics, 1978;* 1977 data are from Bureau of Labor Statistics, *Employment and Unemployment Trends During 1977, 1978;* 1978 data are from Bureau of Labor Statistics, *Employment and Unemployment during 1978: An Analysis,* 1979; 1979 data are from Bureau of Labor Statistics, *Employment and Unemployment during 1979: An Analysis,* 1980.

1981, similar to the increase shown for all jobs and for all manufacturing jobs.

Women's participation in primary metal industry employment, of which basic steel jobs constitute about two-fifths, has historically been far less than their employment in durable manufacturing jobs in general. Thus, in 1965 women held less than 6 percent of all primary metal jobs, clearly constituting a minority in a traditionally male field. This proportion showed only a minor increase in the following decade. In 1974, the year that the consent decree was signed with major steel companies, the proportion of women in primary metals industries was still less than 8 percent.

Although we do not have steel industry data for earlier years, women held an even smaller share of steel industry jobs in 1977 (7.5 percent) than in primary metals in general (9.0 percent). As the figures in Table 6.1 indicate, there was a noticeable growth in the employment of women in the basic steel industry from 1977 to 1979. How much of this is due to the enactment of consent decree provisions is difficult to determine. Other factors, such as an increase in the number of females in the labor market, could also have played a role. It is clear, however, that the growth is significant, amounting to nearly 20 percent in only two years.

It is equally clear that women's share of steel industry employment has fallen sharply since 1979. By the next year, women accounted for only 7.1 percent of the work force, and their absolute numbers were less than they were in 1977. Total industry employment was dropping sharply at the same time, yet the relative share of women was decreasing at an ever faster rate. This fall in share of total jobs is primarily due to the seniority-based layoff system that is almost universal in the steel industry. Thus, as many have observed before, last hired means first fired.

More recent figures, were they available, would undoubtedly show continued erosion in women's representation in the industry. Such trends dramatically show the crucial role of the industry's overall economic situation in determining employment prospects for women. The newer technologies being developed to produce steel, such as the electric furnace and continuous casting (see Chapter 4), require fewer "brute strength" jobs, and thus are more suitable for women than were most jobs associated with earlier technologies in these industries. Further, the 1974 steel industry consent decree and other affirmative action and equal employment opportunity programs have put pressure on the industry to hire more women. None of these factors, however, can offset the negative consequences of declining industry employment on prospects for women. It is within this context that the following more detailed figures must be considered.

FEMALE EMPLOYMENT
IN THE STUDY PLANTS

Most of the data for this study are from two large integrated steel plants. As noted in Chapter 5, these plants employed a combined total of approximately 34,000 workers in 1979. By way of perspective, national figures for employment in the steel industry in 1979 were 453,181 (American Iron and Steel Institute, 1982). Hence, employment in the two study plants constituted approximately 7.5 percent of all such workers in 1979.

As mentioned earlier, the steel industry consent decrees were signed in 1974. One of the two plants in the study was a signatory to this decree. The other company in the study withdrew from consent decree negotiations on the grounds that they had not discriminatorily hired or placed. This company did, however, subsequently sign two conciliation agreements with the Equal Employment Opportunity Commission following four years of negotiations. Yet one of these agreements is not fully operative due to collective bargaining agreement restrictions concerning the accelerated craft placement for women and minorities. Provisions that would revise pertinent seniority limitations are awaiting the signature of the United Steelworkers Union. (Differences between these two companies will be noted in later analysis.)

An initial view of male and female employment in the two study plants, for the period from 1976 to 1979, is provided in Table 6.2. These figures represent the total employment in the two plants, including both hourly and salaried employees. During this period, it should be noted, the absolute numbers of both male and female employees increased, commensurate with rising employment in the companies as a whole. In terms of percentages, women's share of total employment increased by nearly 50 percent. The figure of 12.2 percent female employment may be slightly misleading, however, in that it includes not only blue-collar workers, but workers in salaried positions as well—managerial personnel and, particularly in the case of women, office and clerical workers.

Table 6.3 presents figures for the same years for workers in production and maintenance jobs only—basically what are often called blue-collar jobs, held by workers who belong to the labor union. As can be seen in this table, representation of women in the labor force is less when the salaried employees are removed. In this case, however, the growth of women during the four-year period was even more dramatic, as their numbers increased from 763 in 1976 to 1938 in 1979. Once again, the absolute numbers of males employed also increased during this period, although at a much slower rate, and their relative percentage of the labor force necessarily decreased.

TABLE 6.2 Total, Male and Female Employment in Two Selected Midwest Steel Mills, 1976–79

		Male		Female	
	Total	No.	%	No.	%
1976	30,389	27,901	91.8	2488	8.2
1977	31,444	28,527	90.7	2917	9.3
1978	32,478	28,930	89.1	3548	10.9
1979	34,097	29,929	87.8	4168	12.2

TABLE 6.3 Total, Male and Female Employment in Production and Maintenance Positions in Two Selected Midwest Steel Mills, 1976–79

		Male		Female	
	Total	#	%	#	%
1976	22,100	21,337	96.6	763	3.5
1977	22,843	21,796	95.4	1047	4.6
1978	23,603	22,084	93.6	1519	6.4
1979	24,912	22,974	92.2	1938	7.8

TABLE 6.4 Total Male and Female Craft Employment in Two Selected Midwest Steel Mills, 1976–79

		Male		Female	
	Total	No.	%	No.	%
1976	7332	7305	99.6	27	0.4
1977	7826	7760	99.2	66	0.8
1978	8170	8016	98.3	154	1.7
1979	8780	8583	97.8	197	2.2

Note: Company A 1979 data are for December 31. All other data are for June 30 of each year.

It will be recalled that the steel industry consent decrees placed special emphasis on the craft occupations. And indeed, craft occupations play a major role in steel production, accounting for nearly 35 percent of the production and maintenance workers in the two companies. As can be seen in Table 6.4, women are a distinct minority in these fields. In 1976, shortly after the consent decree was signed, there were only 27 female craft workers out of a total of more than 7000. From one perspective, the increase in female craft workers between 1976 and 1979 was considerable—in terms of absolute numbers, the increase was more than sevenfold. Yet from another perspective, the increase seems less impressive. During that period, more than 1400 craft workers were added to the rolls. Of that number, only 170 were women. As the percentages indicate, women continued to be a distinct minority in these fields, in part perhaps reflecting the greater training time necessary for entrance into the craft occupations. (More discussion of the particular character of craft training is contained in Chapter 9)

Thus there is clear evidence that female employment in the steel plants that we studied did increase in the years following the consent decree. How much of this increase can be attributed specifically to these agreements, however, is impossible to determine with certainty. Conversations with managers at the plants certainly suggest that the governmental pressure accelerated the hiring of women. At the same time, there is evidence that some increase in female hiring predated the consent decrees. In fact, one superintendent reported that his company had begun to hire women for traditionally male jobs in the early 1970s because of difficulty in obtaining adequate numbers of qualified male applicants. It is probably safe to conclude that some increases in female employment would have occurred without any government intervention. At the same time, it seems equally clear that policy decisions accelerated that increase, as discussion in the following section will show.

DETAILED EMPLOYMENT ANALYSIS: SEX AND ETHNICITY

Although the primary concern in this research was the employment pattern for women, such a focus should not preclude consideration of the impact of affirmative action policies for women on other groups of employees. Increased hiring of one group may predictably affect other groups currently employed. From a subjective stance, workers of other sex and ethnic groups may feel disfavored as the newer policies are enacted. In more objective terms, quotas for one group must necessarily affect the relative strength of other groups.

In this section, we present a detailed analysis of employment data, analyzed separately for company, sex, ethnic group and occupational category. Such comparisons may provide some insight into the effects of targeting policies. The reason for separate consideration of the broad occupational groups is that affirmative action targeting may affect different broad occupational groups in different ways. In the case of the steel industry, consent decrees were aimed exclusively at hourly workers, largely the blue-collar jobs.

The white-collar workers in these plants are divided into two groups for analysis—nonexempt and exempt. "Nonexempt" employees are those who are covered by the Fair Labor Standards Act and who must be compensated extra for working extended hours. Over 80 percent of the nonexempt workers in these plants were clerical. The remainder were in such technical occupations as draftsman and computer operator. "Exempt" workers are those not subject to the requirement that they be given additional compensation for working extended hours. The exempt category includes supervisors, managers, and professional workers such as engineers and accountants.

The two companies will be considered separately in these analyses because they were under somewhat different guidelines. Plant A, the larger of the two companies, was not a party to the original consent decree but later signed conciliation agreements. Plant B, the smaller of the two firms, was a party to the original agreement. Data were available from plant A for the period from 1965 to 1980, for hourly, nonexempt, and exempt employees. For plant B, only hourly employee data were available, and these covered only the period from 1973 to 1979.

Hourly Employment, Plant A

Figures 6.1, 6.2, and 6.3 show the total employment for each of the three broad occupational groups as of June 30 each year, together with the percentage of jobs held by various sex and ethnic subgroups. Hourly employment figures, presented in Figure 6.1, are also summarized in Table 6.5. Taken together, these numbers show the course of hourly employment in this particular plant over a 16-year period. During this time, the plant was subject to various equal opportunity and affirmative action programs. At the beginning of the period, the plant was of course covered by the Civil Rights Act of 1964 and Executive Order 11246. The plant was also part of a larger firm that had signed the basic steel industry "Plans for Progress" in 1965 and during the next few years. Although changes in the sex and ethnic composition of employment over this period may not have been due entirely to affirmative action pressures, comments of company officials made it clear that such factors played a role in hiring practices.

The analysis of employment changes in these plants focuses on

FIGURE 6.1 Plant A Hourly Employment by Sex-Ethnic Group Shares June 30, 1965–80

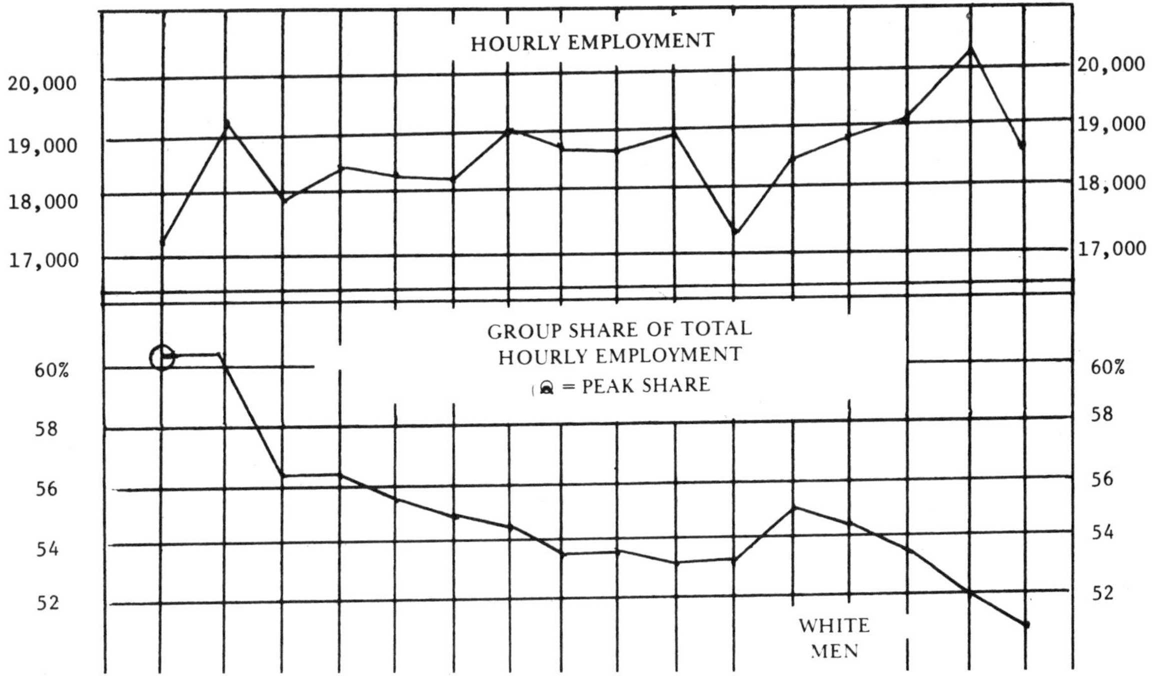

HOURLY EMPLOYMENT

20,000

19,000

18,000

17,000

GROUP SHARE OF TOTAL HOURLY EMPLOYMENT
(● = PEAK SHARE)

60%

58

56

54

52

WHITE MEN

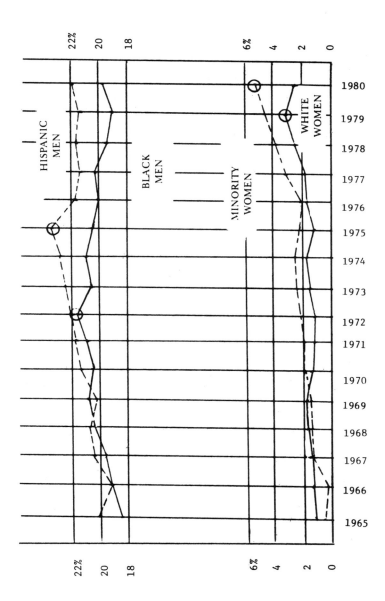

FIGURE 6.2   Plant A Nonexempt Employment by Sex-Ethnic Group Shares June 30, 1965–80

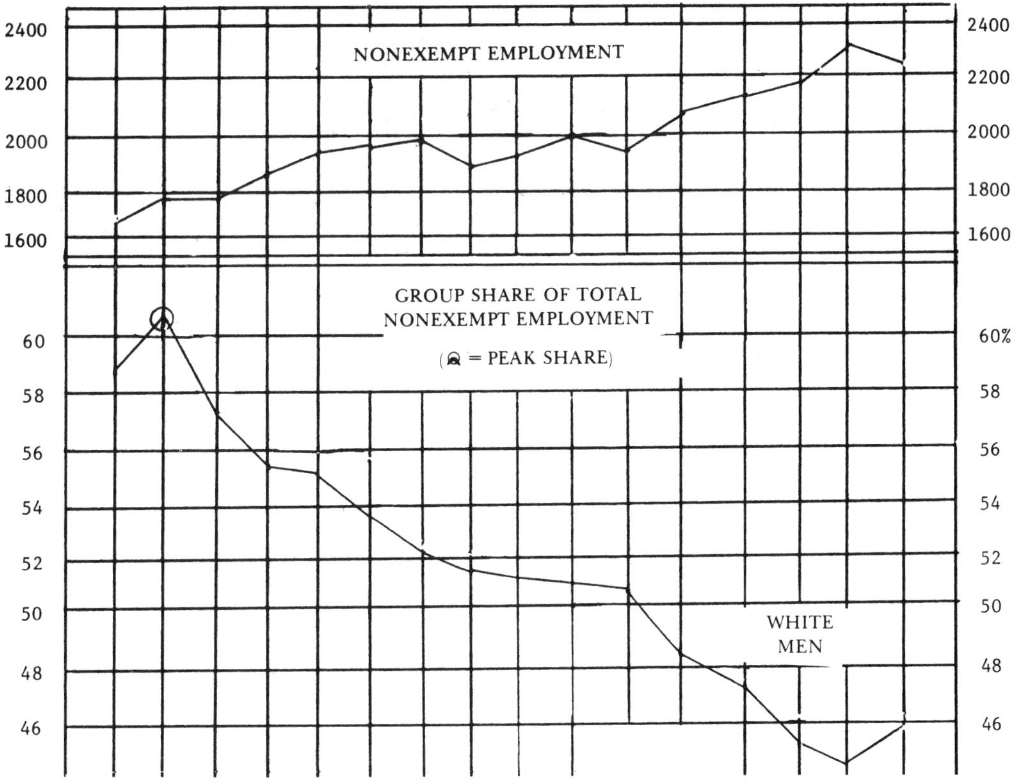

NONEXEMPT EMPLOYMENT

GROUP SHARE OF TOTAL
NONEXEMPT EMPLOYMENT

(⊚ = PEAK SHARE)

WHITE
MEN

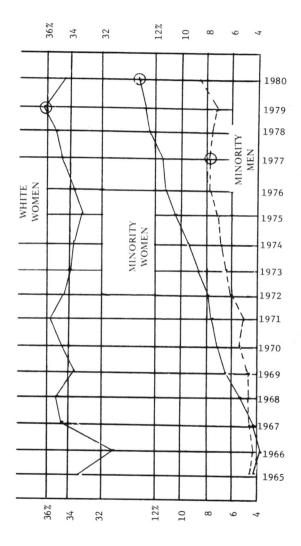

FIGURE 6.3 Plant A Exempt Employment by Sex-Ethnic Group Shares
June 30, 1965–80

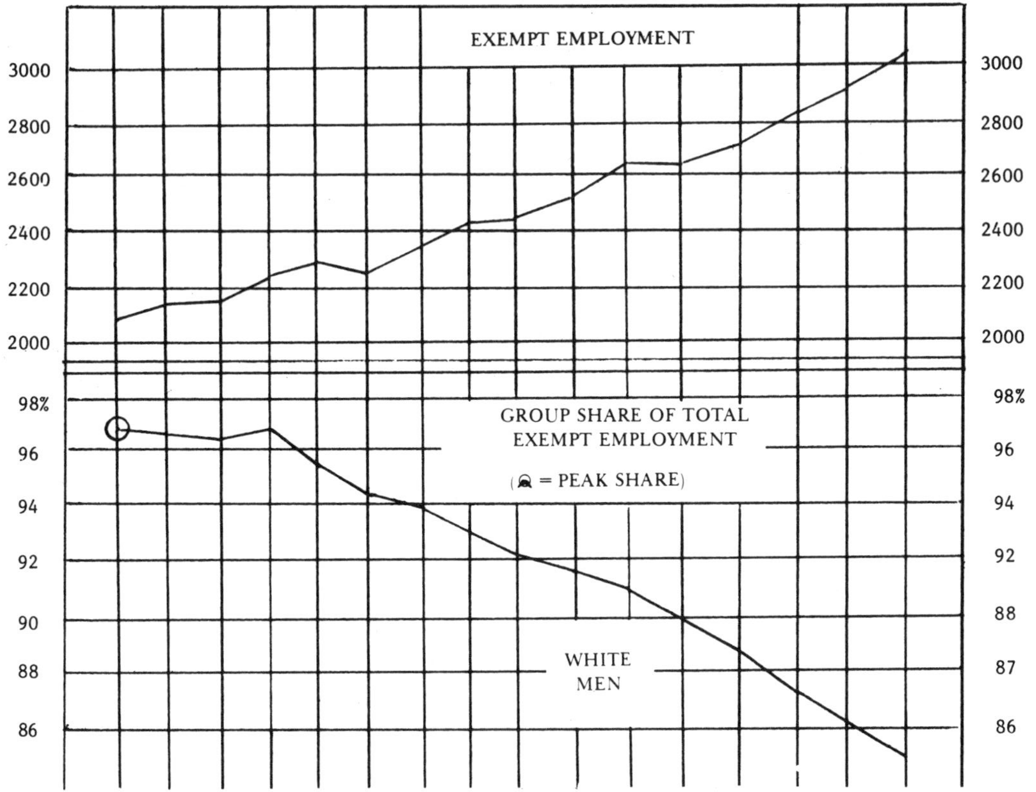

EXEMPT EMPLOYMENT

GROUP SHARE OF TOTAL
EXEMPT EMPLOYMENT

(● = PEAK SHARE)

WHITE
MEN

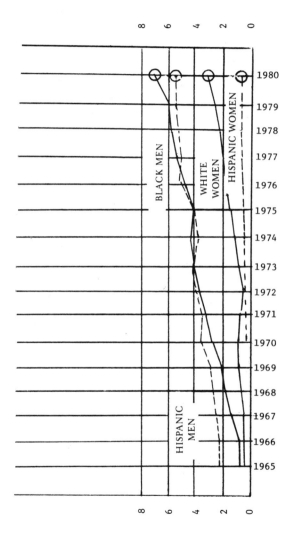

TABLE 6.5   Plant A Hourly Employment in 1965 and 1980

	1965	1980	Change
Total Hourly Employment	17,204	18,692	+1488
Number of jobs held by			
White men	10,344	9,626	−715
Black men	3,179	3,653	+474
Hispanic men	3,447	4,108	+661
White women	184	453	+269
Minority women[a]	50	849	+799
Percent of total jobs held by			
White men	60.0	51.6	−8.4
Black men	18.4	19.4	+1.0
Hispanic men	20.0	22.0	+2.0
White women	1.2	2.4	+1.2
Minority women	0.4	4.6	+4.2

[a] Blacks and Hispanics are combined in these tables when their individual numbers are too small to warrant separation.

proportions of jobs held by various groups. In this way, changes in total employment due to shifts in the output of the plant and levels of the economy are eliminated as a source of change. However, it is important to remember that because employment in these plants grew through most of the study period, the *number* of jobs held by various sex and ethnic groups generally increased throughout the period.

The employment share, that is, the proportion, of black and Hispanic females and males rose slightly during the period from 1965 to 1970, and the relative employment of white women was constant. White men were the only group whose share of the total employment dropped during this period. The minority male share of total employment peaked in the early 1970s and remained flat until 1976. This was a period of stable employment in the plant, and this condition probably reduced opportunities to increase the minority share of employment. The share of total jobs held by both minority and white females was also stable through the early and middle 1970s.

Reflecting the 1975 recession, total employment in this plant dropped by about 10 percent (approximately 1700) from 1974 to 1975, then rose steadily to 1979. It is interesting to note the changes in the relative employment of various subgroups in this period, especially in view of the shifting emphasis of public policy in the equal opportunity/affirmative action area.

As employment rose after 1975, the white male share of the total first rose, and then resumed its long-term decline. This temporary increase was primarily due to the recall of laid-off workers; white males were recalled in disproportionate numbers because they tended to have greater seniority than other sex-ethnic groups. After 1975, the female share of jobs rose at a rapid rate, although remaining at low absolute levels, an effect which can probably be attributed to affirmative action requirements newly incumbent on the steel industry. For minority males, despite an increase in absolute numbers, there was some decrease in relative proportion of total jobs.

In an effort to assess more specifically the impact of the consent decrees, a further analysis was undertaken. This analysis compares the annual change in the sex-ethnic composition of employment during the years before women were targeted for affirmative action with the post-targeting changes in sex-ethnic composition. Average annual change in the share of total employment is computed for each sex-ethnic category. The base period is 1973 to 1976, the period just before Company A accepted the conciliation agreement requiring that 20 percent of newly hired employees be women. The postperiod is 1976 to 1979, the first three years after targeting women.

As Table 6.6 shows, the impact of targeting women is dramatic. In the pretargeting period, there was virtually no change in female employment, whereas both numeric and percentage increases in the posttargeting period are substantial. Minority males lost ground in terms of their share of total employment in both periods. The 1974–75 recession probably accounts for the pretargeting decline; relative posttargeting declines may be associated with the increased emphasis on hiring women. White males also showed a proportional decline in the posttargeting period.

Nonexempt Employment, Plant A

Trends in the nonexempt work force are shown in Figure 2; specific comparisons between 1965 and 1980 are shown in Table 6.7. The picture here is similar to that of the hourly employees: white women and all minority groups gained in both absolute numbers and in relative share of the employment force. White men, although increasing slightly in numbers, represented a smaller share of total employment in 1980. It should be recalled that nonexempt employees were not specifically covered by the conciliation agreements. Thus it is perhaps not surprising that the relative gains of women in the posttargeting period were not markedly greater than in the pretargeting period, as indicated by Table 6.8, particularly when compared with the patterns of the hourly employees.

TABLE 6.6 Pretargeting and Posttargeting Employment Plant A Hourly Employees

	Males			Females			
	White	*Black*	*Hispanic*	*White*	*Black*	*Hispanic*	*Total*
Pretargeting (1973–76)							
(1) 1976 actual employment	10,043	3715	3997	271	238	107	616
(2) 1976 employment if same percent of total as in 1973	9,947	3784	4134	276	239	92	607
(3) Difference: (1) − (2)	+196	−69	−137	−5	−1	+15	+9
(4) Percent gain or loss in period	+2.0	−1.8	−3.3	−1.8	−0.4	+16.3	+1.5
(5) Average annual gain or loss (percent)	+0.7	−0.6	−1.1	−0.6	−0.1	+5.5	+0.5
Posttargeting (1976–79)							
(1) 1979 actual employment	10,516	3925	4272	598	586	334	1518
(2) 1979 employment if same percent of total as in 1976	11,066	4066	4410	324	263	101	688
(3) Difference: (1) − (2)	−550	−141	−138	+274	+323	+233	+830
(4) Percent gain or loss in period	−5.0	−3.5	−3.10	+84.0	+122.8	+230.7	+120.6
(5) Average annual gain or loss (percent)	−1.7	−1.2	−1.0	+28.2	+40.9	+76.9	+40.2

TABLE 6.7   Plant A Nonexempt Employment in 1965 and 1980

	1965	1980	Change
Total nonexempt employment	1648	2153	+505
Number of jobs held by			
White men	969	1013	+44
Minority men	65	161	+96
White women	549	756	+207
Minority women	65	223	+158
Percent of jobs held by			
White men	58.8	47.1	−11.7
Minority men	3.9	7.5	+3.6
White women	33.3	35.1	+1.8
Minority women	3.9	10.3	+6.4

Exempt Employment, Plant A

Changes in the sex and ethnic composition of the work force at Plant A were also considered for the exempt employment class, primarily managerial and professional jobs. Again, these are jobs that were not covered by the conciliation agreements. As Table 6.9 indicates, this class was almost exclusively occupied by white males in 1965. Nearly a 50 percent increase in the number of exempt employees between 1965 and 1980 allowed for some significant changes in the numbers of women and minority group members. The number of white women in these positions increased by a factor of 7; the number of Hispanic men increased by a factor of 13. As a result of these changes, the relative share of white males decreased from 1965 to 1980; in absolute numbers, however, white males obtained over three-fifths of the exempt jobs added between 1965 and 1980. It should also be noted that in 1980, white males still accounted for nearly 86 percent of the managerial and professional employment, and males in general, combined across ethnic groups, constituted more than 97 percent.

There are a number of possible reasons for the slower growth rate for women in exempt groups as compared to hourly employees. First, the conciliation agreements did not apply to this class and thus the impetus to hire women may have been less. Second, a greater "lead time" may be needed to increase the numbers of previously underrepresented groups, given the longer educational and training periods associated with higher-level jobs. Until rather recently, for example, the numbers of women and minority men graduating in engineering and other technical fields has been quite small. Further, the demand for women in these fields has increased greatly in recent years, and steel companies have difficulty competing with firms in more glamorous industries for these scarce workers.

TABLE 6.8 Pretargeting and Posttargeting Employment Plant A Nonexempt Employees

	Males			Females			
	White	Black	Hispanic	White	Black	Hispanic	Total
Pretargeting (1973–76)							
(1) 1976 actual employment	995	76	80	698	108	109	915
(2) 1976 employment if same percent of total as in 1973	1056	62	70	705	91	83	879
(3) Difference: (1) – (2)	–61	+14	+10	–7	+17	+26	+36
(4) Percent gain or loss in period	–5.8	+22.6	+14.3	–1.0	+18.7	+31.3	+4.1
(5) Average annual gain or loss (percent)	–1.9	+7.5	+4.8	–0.3	+6.2	+10.4	+1.4
Posttargeting (1976–79)							
(1) 1979 actual employment	1018	68	95	822	125	156	1103
(2) 1979 employment if same percent of total as in 1976	1101	85	89	722	119	121	1012
(3) Difference: (1) – (2)	–83	–17	+6	+50	+6	+35	+91
(4) Percent gain or loss in period	–7.5	–20.0	+6.7	+6.5	+5.0	+28.9	+9.0
(5) Average annual gain or loss (percent)	–2.5	–6.7	+2.2	+2.2	+1.7	+9.6	+3.0

Combining all jobs at Plant A, white males lost 715 hourly jobs, but gained 44 nonexempt and 577 exempt jobs from 1965 to 1980. This pattern represents a net decline of 94 jobs, but a substantial gain in high-level jobs. White women gained 547 jobs in the same time period, approximately half of which were hourly while only 71 were at the managerial level. Black and Hispanic males also showed strong gains during the period, obtaining 698 and 879 jobs, respectively, the majority of which were at the hourly level. In absolute numbers, the largest gainers during this period were minority women, who registered an increase of 969 jobs;[1] 82 percent of these were in the hourly work force and only 1 percent were at the exempt level.

Hourly Employment, Plant B

Fewer data were available to us at Plant B. We had access to employment figures only for the hourly work force, and only for the period from 1973 to 1979. These figures are presented in Table 6-10 and are represented graphically in Figure 6.4. The analysis of targeting effects is shown in Table 6.11.

The pattern at Plant B is somewhat different from that at Plant A. During this six-year period, all groups increased in absolute number, reflecting the sharp growth in employment at this company from 1973 to 1979—nearly a 33 percent increase in the hourly work force. Relatively speaking, the growth of women and minority male subgroups was larger as their numbers doubled and tripled in this period. Table 6.11 confirms the fact that women and minority male hourly employees at Plant B gained in employment shares throughout the period of study. Both black and Hispanic men increased their share of total jobs more rapidly in the posttargeting period than in the pretargeting period. In contrast, women, who were the specific focus of the targeting policies during this period, did not show an increase in the relative proportion of jobs they held, despite substantial changes in numbers. At the same time, it should be noted that women were increasing at a rapid rate even in the pretargeting period, suggesting that some increase in hiring of women may have occurred prior to, and independently of, the specific consent decree provisions. (As noted earlier, informal conversation with plant personnel suggested that this indeed was the case.)

Hourly Employment in the Industry

Further consideration of the impact of affirmative action policies on the employment of women, as well as the possibility of adverse impact on other groups, is provided by inspection of industry-wide figures. Data were obtained from the Equal Employment Opportunity Commission for the

TABLE 6.9 Plant A Exempt Employment in 1965 and 1980

	1965	1980	Change
Total exempt employment	2074	3021	+947
Number of jobs held by			
White men	2015	2592	+577
Black men	37	190	+153
Hispanic men	12	156	+144
White women	10	71	+61
Minority women	—	12	+12
Percent of jobs held by			
White men	97.2	85.8	−11.4
Black men	1.8	6.3	+4.5
Hispanic men	0.6	5.1	+4.5
White women	0.5	2.4	+1.9
Minority women	—	0.4	+0.4

TABLE 6.10 Plant B Hourly Employment in 1973 and 1979

	1973	1979	Change
Total hourly employment	4603	6190	+1587
Number of jobs held by			
White men	3864	4426	+562
Minority men	449	880	+431
White women	130	484	+354
Minority women	160	400	+240
Percent of jobs held by			
White men	83.9	71.5	−12.4
Minority men	9.7	14.2	+4.5
White women	2.8	7.8	+5.0
Minority women	3.5	6.5	+3.0

TABLE 6.11 Pretargeting and Posttargeting Employment Plant B Hourly Employees

	Males			Females			Total
	White	Black	Hispanic	White	Black	Hispanic	
Pretargeting (1973–74)							
(1) 1974 actual employment	3997	390	79	175	201	2	378
(2) 1974 employment if same percent of total as in 1973	4069	379	78	140	174	3	317
(3) Difference: (1) − (2)	−72	+11	+1	+35	+27	−1	+61
(4) Percent gain or loss in period (3) − (2)	−1.8	+3.0	+1.2	+25.0	+15.5	*	+19.29
(5) Average annual gain or loss (percent)	−1.8	+3.0	+1.2	+25.0	+15.5	*	+19.2
Posttargeting (1974–79)							
(1) 1979 actual employment	4375	726	140	479	398	7	884
(2) 1979 employment if same percent of total as in 1974	5053	496	98	220	257	2	479
(3) Difference: (1) − (2)	−678	+230	+42	+259	+141	+5	+405
(4) Percent gain or loss in period (3) − (2)	−13.4	+46.4	+42.9	+117.7	+54.9	*	+84.6
(5) Average annual gain or loss (percent)	−2.7	+9.3	+8.6	+23.5	+11.0	*	+16.9

*Numbers too small for meaningful analysis.

FIGURE 6.4 Plant B Hourly Employment by Sex-Ethnic Group Shares June 30, 1973–79

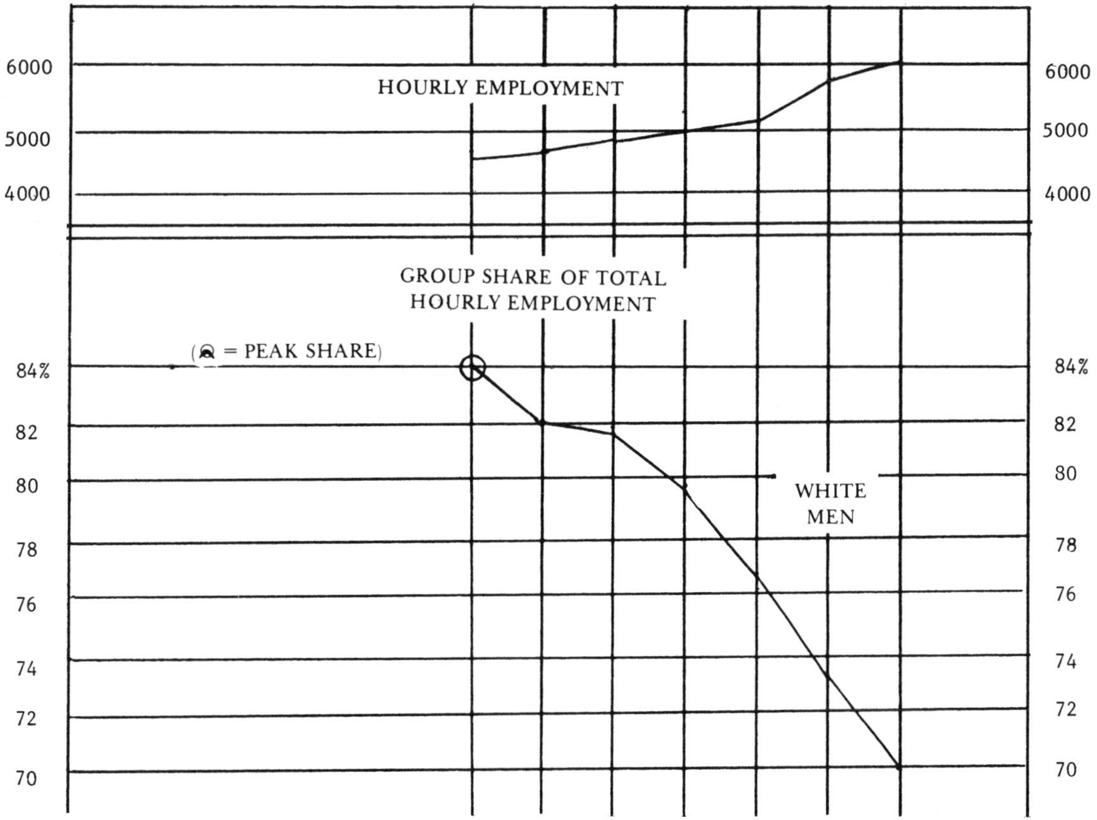

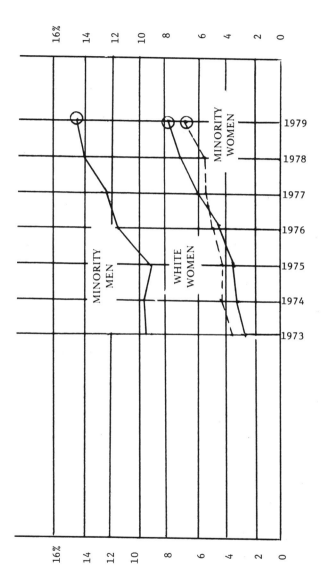

years 1966, 1974, and 1978.[2] These data were divided by sex and ethnic group, were based on reports sent by the industries to the Commission on a periodic basis, and were available for specific industries. For this analysis, we concentrated on the industry group entitled Blast Furnaces and Basic Steel Production. This category covered 534 plants in 1966, 614 plants in 1974, and 654 plants in 1978. Because the plants included in the survey in the various years were not identical, caution must be used in comparing data for the different years. Further caution is warranted because all plants in this survey were not subject to the 1974 consent decree concerning the hiring of women. Nonetheless, these figures may provide some indication, albeit rough, of the effects of targeting on the employment of women and other groups.

Table 6.12 presents the figures for the employment of women and of minorities in the pretargeting period (1966–74) and in the posttargeting period (1974–78), for both women and for minority males. As a point of comparison, data on total blue-collar employment in the United States is shown as well. As can be seen in this table, blue-collar employment of women increased more rapidly in the steel industry than in overall blue-collar employment, both in the pretargeting and in the posttargeting period. In the posttargeting period, this increase is particularly striking, as the population of women in this industry grew nearly three times as rapidly as in the pretargeting period. In contrast, there was no such explosive growth in employment of blue-collar women generally in the posttargeting period.

As these figures also indicate, minority men did not have a decline in their relative share of jobs during the period that targeting policies were directed at women. Although their growth was certainly not as spectacular, they continued to make gains in the posttargeting period, and, in fact, their rate of growth accelerated during this period. Whereas women gained nearly 8,000 jobs in the steel industry from 1974 to 1978, minority men gained more than 10,000 jobs.

SUMMARY

It is clear that the number of women employed in blue-collar jobs in the basic steel industry increased sharply in the late 1970s. Although we can not point with assurance to the consent decrees as the only cause, it seems quite certain that they were at least partially responsible. Female employment in a broader sample of blue-collar jobs, encompassing a large number of industries that were not subject to government regulation, did not show the same growth rate. This is not to deny that other factors may be contributory. For example, in one plant that we studied, increasing

TABLE 6.12 U.S. Total and SIC Industry 331 Blue-Collar Employment

	U.S.		SIC 331		
	Total	Female	Total	Female	Minority Male
Pretargeting (1966–74)					
(1) 1974 actual employment	29,776,000	5,195,000	373,910	6,911	70,302
(2) 1974 employment if same percent as in 1966	—	4,913,000	—	3,739	63,939
(3) Difference: row (1) − row (2)	—	282,000	—	3,172	6,363
(4) Percent gain or loss in period row (3) ÷ (2)	—	5.7	—	84.8	10.0
(5) Average annual gain (percent)	—	0.7	—	10.6	1.2
Posttargeting (1974–78)					
(1) 1978 actual employment	31,531,000	5,767,000	383,882	14,711	80,395
(2) 1978 employment if same percent of total as in 1974	—	5,486,000	—	6,910	72,170
(3) Difference: row (1) − row (2)	—	281,000	—	7,801	8,225
(4) Percent gain or loss in period: row (3) ÷ (2)	—	5.1	—	112.9	11.4
(5) Average annual gain (percent)	—	1.3	—	28.2	2.8

Source: U.S. data from Bureau of Labor Statistics, 1976 and Bureau of Labor Statistics, 1980; SIC 331 data from Equal Employment Opportunity Commission, 1980.

numbers of women were being hired before the consent decrees were signed, presumably the result of labor market factors.

From a policy perspective, it is important to consider the potential effects of targeting one particular group, in this case women, on the employment status of other groups. If more women are hired, does that mean a setback for other groups that were previously the object of concern, such as minority males? Although there is certainly no simple answer to that question, our data indicate that such a decrement did not generally occur. In a national sample, minority males showed proportional growth in the posttargeting period, as they did in one of our two study plants. In the other study plant, the proportion of jobs held by minority males decreased slightly, although there was some increase in absolute numbers.

Differences in these patterns are determined by a number of factors. First, it is important to consider the relative strength of various groups prior to the new policy initiatives. For example, in the case of company A, minority males constituted 43.5 percent of the total employment prior to the consent agreements. In contrast, minority males accounted for only 9.7 percent of the employment at company B and 18.6 percent of the total employment in the national sample that we obtained from EEOC. Consequently, consideration of relative growth or decline must take into account the base from which such changes developed.

A second factor of major importance is the growth rate in the industry or the particular plant itself. To the extent that overall employment is increasing, it is quite possible to increase the proportion of members of a previously underrepresented group without harming the progress of previously targeted groups. Should employment not be increasing, however, the situation is a much more difficult one. When jobs are limited, preference for members of one group may well mean disadvantage for other groups.

The overall employment picture is particularly important when we consider the current state of the steel industry. Although women made noticeable gains in the five years following the consent decrees, this progress has been totally wiped out by the recessionary effects of the early 1980s. The percentage of women employed in the steel industry is now less than it was prior to the consent decrees, and the numbers are drastically smaller as well. Because seniority affects layoffs, in an industry that is currently operating at considerably less than 50 percent of capacity, recently hired women are among the first to be laid off. The future of the steel industry when the recessionary period ends is a matter of considerable speculation. Although most would agree that many workers will eventually be rehired, it appears likely that employment in the basic steel industry will never recover its former levels. Should there be such a fallback, it will be difficult for women to make inroads as rapidly as they did in the late 1970s.

Whether, and how soon, women become a major segment of the blue-collar work force in the steel mills is in part a function of the economy and the status of the steel industry within that national economic picture. The status of women also depends on their performance within the mills while they were working, and their reactions to that work. It is to this topic that the next three chapters are devoted.

NOTES

1. Minority women are especially desirable hires from a viewpoint of affirmative action targets, because they are members of two protected classes. In the special parlance of the personnel field, minority women are often referred to as "twofers," as in two-for-the-price-of-one.

2. We appreciate the cooperation of Ms. Betty Wright of the Statistical Survey Branch of the Equal Employment Opportunity commission in providing these data.

7

Women in
the Steel Mill:
Performance

The bottom line, as many would say, is whether women can do the job. Although other issues, such as attitudes, barriers, aspirations, and job satisfaction are important, we begin with the question that is paramount in the minds of the industry management, and in the minds of many outside commentators as well. Can women do the work required in this traditionally male field?

To answer this question, it is first important to know just what "the job" is. Even that question is not a simple one, as there are many different jobs in the steel industry. Therefore we will begin with a description of some of the basic jobs in the industry, followed by an assessment of the requirements of those jobs from the workers themselves.

We will then look at the performance of women from the perspective of supervisory personnel, using objective indices when possible (such as turnover and absence data), and relying on subjective appraisals when objective indices are not available. Then we will consider these same questions from the viewpoint of the male workers. Finally, we will turn to the female workers themselves, to determine just how well they think women are doing.

STEEL MILL JOBS

The sheer size and scope of a large integrated steel plant necessarily means that there is no simple description of the work done there. Even excluding the exempt and nonexempt personnel, the jobs in a steel mill are incredibly diverse.

Perhaps it is useful to begin with a brief description of the skills, job requirements, and work environments associated with the various stages of the steelmaking process. As discussed in Chapter 4, steel production can be described in terms of a sequence of stages, beginning with the making of raw iron and steel and ending with finished steel products.

In the initial stage, coke is produced by heating coal in long batteries of vertical ovens. Jobs at this stage tend to be extremely dirty and unpleasant; workers are surrounded by the dust and fumes of the coke ovens. Craft workers, operators, and laborers are all involved at this stage, operating and repairing equipment in the coke oven batteries and the cars that move the finished coke to the next stage.

Iron ore, coke, and limestone are then mixed in a blast furnace to produce molten iron. Again, the environmental factors at this stage are significant, with heat, dust, and fumes in evidence throughout. At the next stage, molten iron is combined with other alloys to make steel. Here workers are surrounded by enormous equipment and the temperatures are very high. Laboring jobs may involve shoveling slag, transporting materials, and charging the furnace for a burn. Other more technical jobs include those of the chemists who take samples of the molten steel to test it for the proper composition. The pace of work is irregular in many of these jobs. Unlike the auto assembly line, steelmaking is often a process of starts and stops, of charging the elements and then waiting until the mixture has reached the proper specifications.

After the steel is made, it is converted to semifinished forms, called blooms, billets and slabs. Again, there are a variety of jobs required at this stage of the sequence. Laboring jobs may involve shoveling slag that has been shaved from the ingots. Operating jobs are often performed within air-conditioned booths, regulating the shaping of ingots through mechanical and computer-assisted equipment.

At the finishing end of the process, steel is shaped into specific products: sheets, plates, and rolls. Great precision is required to assure that the finished products meet specifications—specifications that can be varied by a fraction of an inch depending on the ultimate destination. On the whole, jobs at the finishing end are "cleaner" jobs: more air-conditioned facilities are available, there is less dust and fumes, and fewer physical demands are present. Some workers, for example, are primarily involved in marking finished bundles and cataloging the supply. Others may operate machinery or mobile equipment that moves supplies from one location to another. As in every other department, large numbers of craft workers are required for the maintenance of the equipment and the machinery, a process that continues 24 hours a day throughout the week.

Because the steel plant is in continuous operation, a work force must be there at all times. Consequently, workers operate on shifts, with three eight-hour shifts per day. For some workers, these shifts remain constant and a worker may, depending upon his or her job, always work a 7 A.M. to 3 P.M. shift, to cite just one example. More often, however, workers are on alternating or rotating schedules, working 7 A.M. to 3 P.M. one week, 3 P.M. to 11 P.M. the next week, and 11 P.M. to 7 A.M. the following week.

Jobs within the steel mills cut across these various departments and are as diverse as the departments themselves. In our study, we have focused on eight principal categories, which accounted for nearly all of the jobs that we encountered in our interviews. These jobs are listed and described in Table 7.1. The first two of these job categories exemplify the skilled craft worker, two among dozens of craft workers in the typical steel mill that comprise roughly one-third of the plant blue-collar workers. These two are representative of the crafts in that they are two of the most important crafts in the industry. Craft jobs require substantial training, usually obtained either through a formal apprentice program (typically four years in length) or through a less formal handyman-helper arrangement of indefinite duration. More detailed analysis of the craft occupations will be found in Chapter 9.

Other job categories listed represent semiskilled or operative positions, such as mobile equipment operators and machine operators. These are typically not entry-level positions, although neither do they require the formal apprentice training demanded in craft occupations. Generally they are less physically but more mentally demanding than labor positions. They pay a somewhat higher wage than do labor jobs, and they often carry more prestige.

Labor is typically the entry-level job in the steel industry, and it includes a variety of manual activities. Janitorial work is usually classified as one of the labor jobs, although we have separated it in our analysis because the job requirements are somewhat different (and, as we have seen, the occupants of that job more often are women). Both the labor and the operative jobs can be grouped under the broader title of production jobs, distinguishing them from the craft occupations.

REQUIREMENTS OF STEEL MILL JOBS

Given the diversity of jobs, it is difficult to identify the requirements of a "typical" steel mill job. Furthermore, the exact requirements of each job are rarely specified, although in-house personnel in some companies have been attempting to formulate clearer job descriptions in recent years. Among labor jobs in particular, the range of activities is considerable and

**TABLE 7.1   Principal Job Categories of Workers
Included in Interview Study
(hourly workers)**

Millwright/vocational mechanic
Skilled craft worker, helper, or apprentice who inspects, repairs, replaces, installs, adjusts, and maintains a wide variety of mechanical equipment.

Motor inspector
Skilled craft worker or apprentice who inspects, repairs, replaces, installs, adjusts, and maintains all electrical equipment. Also makes certain mechanical repairs, as required, in connection with electrical services.

Clerical jobs
Jobs with various titles involving primarily writing, recording, computing, or marking.

Mobile equipment operator
Semiskilled worker who operates such moving equipment as fork lift trucks on which he or she typically rides while operating.

Janitor
Unskilled job involving primarily cleaning and housekeeping tasks.

Checker or stocker
Semiskilled job involving checking tools or stocking supplies, generally from a fixed location.

Machine operator
Semiskilled job operating a variety of stationary machinery.

Labor
Unskilled jobs covering wide variety of activities, requiring primarily physical effort.

may vary from day to day, depending on production demands. To get some idea of what different jobs entailed, we simply asked each of the workers that we interviewed what kinds of physical activities he or she did during the course of an average day. Lifting was mentioned most often, by nearly 60 percent of both male and female workers. Other activities mentioned less frequently, generally by about 20 percent of the workers, were pushing, digging, walking, sweeping, and climbing. These latter activities tend to be more job-specific. Sweeping, for example, is most likely to be part of a janitorial job; digging slag is a component of more typical labor jobs.

Perhaps more crucial than the general type of activity are the specific strength demands that a job entails. It is around this issue that many of the debates as to women's suitability for hard-hatted jobs circle, with the frequent assumption being that women simply do not have the physical strength to perform adequately.

As noted earlier, women on the average have less physical strength than do men. The significance of this difference may be debated, however. First, the absence of specific physical strength testing in the companies that we studied does not allow us to say whether the women we studied were necessarily weaker than the men and whether they do, in fact, approximate the national average for females. Second, it is important to document just what the strength demands of the jobs are. The lower such demands, the less significant the sex difference in physical capacity becomes.

Our initial inquiries on this issue yielded discrepant opinions. On the one hand, some managers (primarily in the personnel offices) suggested that the physical demands were considerable, thus making the jobs beyond the bounds of many women. At the same time, some floor supervisors that we interviewed suggested that the physical demands are considerably less. As one supervisor observed, "The days of the bull moose are over," while another reported that no one is ever asked to lift more than 50 pounds. (Union agreements in some cases have stipulated a 50-pound weight limit.)

Our own approach was to ask the workers themselves how much strength their jobs required: the weight of the heaviest object they had to lift, the frequency of lifting that object, and a more general assessment of the amount of physical strength required in their jobs.

The range of responses to these questions was considerable. On the one hand, some workers facetiously (but accurately) noted that the heaviest thing they had to lift was either a pencil, their lunch bag, or a hard hat, identifying no physical strains in their jobs whatsoever. At the other extreme, a few workers reported lifting weights of more than 200 pounds, although it was not always clear whether or not these weights were lifted without the help of some equipment or another worker. The typical response to the question concerning the maximum weight lifted was 50 pounds. Fewer than a third of either the women or the men reported ever lifting anything heavier than 75 pounds.

Of equal importance is the fact that most of these maximum physical demands occurred infrequently. More than half of the workers reported that they lifted the heaviest weight only once a day or less. Rare was the worker who reported a frequent need to lift heavy objects. Corroborating these reports, when workers were asked to give a general estimate of the amount of physical strength that their job entailed, the mean response indicated something between "a slight amount" and "quite a bit."

Sheer physical strength is not the only issue of concern. Physical endurance is also critical to many steel mill jobs, which may involve repeated shoveling or constant lifting of lighter weights. Indeed, in our interviews most subjects considered endurance more important than physical strength. Unlike the case with strength, it is not clear that men possess more physical endurance than do women. Indeed, in some respects, women have been found to have more endurance than men do.

Beyond the issues of physical strength and endurance, we questioned both supervisors and workers about a variety of factors that would determine how well a worker did in steel mill jobs. Supervisors, when asked to evaluate the importance of specific characteristics, generally agreed that most of the factors we mentioned were at least somewhat important. Mean ratings of their judgments are shown in Table 7.2, ordered from most to least important.

As can been seen in this table, interpersonal characteristics are rated most highly, in that the four highest ratings are given to worker-worker and worker-supervisor interactions. Endurance is next in line, ranked considerably higher than physical strength. Clearly, supervisors support the view that physical strength is not the paramount requirement to performing steel mill jobs.

Both the male and the female workers were asked a similar set of questions. Their responses are shown in Table 7.3, roughly ordered from the most important to the least important factor. Once again, interpersonal factors are generally believed to be more important that physical strength, training, or experience. Both men and women agree on the greater importance of attitudes, compared with other job factors, as determinants of performance on steel mill jobs.

There were few differences between women and men in their perception of job requirements. Only in two cases were the differences

TABLE 7.2 Mean Importance of Factors Affecting Worker Performance as Rated by Supervisors[a]

Characteristic	Mean
Attitude of worker toward coworkers	3.47
Attitude of immediate supervisor toward worker	3.38
Attitude of worker toward immediate supervisor	3.33
Attitudes of coworkers toward worker	3.16
Physical endurance	3.10
Attitude of department superintendent toward worker	3.05
Ability to deal with hazing	2.74
Physical strength	2.69
Previous work experience	2.59
Vocational training	2.55
Formal education	2.46
Length of time in department	2.39

[a]Ratings made on scale where 1 = not at all important, 2 = slightly important, 3 = quite important, 4 = extremely important.

TABLE 7.3 Mean Importance of Factors Affecting Worker Performance as Rated by Female and Male Workers[a]

	Female Workers	Male Workers	Significance Level of Difference
Attitude toward coworkers	3.35	3.33	N.S.
Attitude of immediate supervisor toward worker	3.11	3.20	N.S.
Attitude of worker toward immediate supervisor	3.10	3.12	N.S.
Attitude of department superintendent toward the worker	2.97	2.96	N.S.
Attitudes of coworkers	2.84	2.90	N.S.
Ability to deal with hazing	2.91	2.92	N.S.
Physical endurance	2.97	2.93	N.S.
Physical strength	2.69	2.62	N.S.
Length of time in department	2.31	2.54	.10
Previous work experience	2.22	2.69	.001
Vocational training	2.09	2.35	.07
Formal education	2.10	2.02	N.S.

[a]Ratings made on scale where 1 = not at all important, 2 = slightly important, 3 = quite important, 4 = extremely important.

significant: men considered previous work experience and vocational training to be more important than women did. Second, men tended to believe that the sheer length of time that a worker had been in the department, than did the women workers. This tendency to impute value to that the men workers who were interviewed tended to have greater previous work experience and vocational training, as well as more time in the department, than did the women workers. This tendency to imput value to some factors on which they had an advantage over women (e.g., time in department) gives extra credibility to the agreement of men with women in assessing the role of physical strength and endurance. Men did not rate these factors more highly than did women, despite a belief that their strength was greater.

Overall, there is a consensus among supervisors, men workers, and women workers that attitudinal factors are the most important determinants of success in steel mill jobs. This finding bodes well for women steel mill workers. Attitudinal factors are not immutable barriers to success, as physical factors may have been had they been paramount.

EVALUATING THE PERFORMANCE OF WOMEN: OBJECTIVE INDICES

When we first approached managers within the steel industry and asked the relatively simple question, "How are women doing?", the answers were diverse. Often, however, we were given negative exemplars—descriptions of one or another woman who had caused problems. Examples of women who had filed grievances, women who let men do all their work, women who only wanted the physically less demanding janitorial jobs—many incidents such as these were described, often in considerable detail. Yet when we looked for specific records and objective measures that might allow us to assess performance, we found little material that was helpful. In the few cases where we pursued the details of critical incidents described by managers, we found little evidence to support the alleged shortcomings of the woman or women in question.

Performance records were not kept systematically on individual workers in these plants. Although foremen may have subjective summaries filed in their heads, it was rarely the case that anything but a brief notation, often for an instance of difficulty, would be recorded on permanent records. Production figures were available for large units—for example, a particular department or in some cases, a particular shift—but these indicators are far too gross to enable one to untangle the specific contribution of women to an increase or decrease in production. Despite considerable thought given to the issue, we were not able to develop a satisfactory measure of productivity that would allow us to assess the performance of women.[1]

Turnover Data

Information was available on turnover within the two companies. Although such an index does not speak directly to the issue of women's performance, it provides useful information regarding the potential costs to the company or the industry in hiring women. Turnover is a major expense factor in employment, estimated to cost American industry as much as $11 billion per year (Augustine, 1972). Costs of turnover include the increased costs for social security and unemployment compensation; underutilized facilities if a replacement is not hired immediately; employment costs, such as interview time and testing expenses; administrative costs of notification and payroll changes; and loss of productivity until the new employee reaches the performance level of the person who left the job.

There is no immediate reason to suspect that turnover would be greater for women than men. Previous studies, for example, have not typically found sex differences in worker turnover (Magione, 1973). Yet in a field that has traditionally been outside the realm of experience for women, it seemed possible that women might be less prepared for the job conditions and demands, and might be more apt to leave than men, who could well have greater familiarity with the job setting prior to employment. Alternatively, more women than men might be terminated before the end of the probationary period, if it was believed that they were incapable of doing the job.

Although the companies that we studied had not calculated comparative indices of turnover, we were able to compute these figures from the available information on employment, hiring, and terminations. We calculated hiring rates in a similar manner, because of previous evidence that turnover and tenure are related (Mobley, Griffith, Hand, & Meglino, 1979). More specifically, terminations tend to be higher among new employees. Thus, one might predict a higher termination rate for women than men in these plants on the basis of tenure alone.

As Table 7.4 shows, that was not the case. The termination rates for women and men did not differ significantly, despite the highly significant differences in hiring rates.[2] Neither did these termination rates differ when separate tests were conducted analyzing white and minority women and men. More precise estimates of turnover would be possible if we had been able to conduct a longitudinal study, matching women and men who were hired at the same time and following them through time to compare termination rates. Even in the absence of such a study, however, it is clear that the termination rate for women is not greater than that for men. Given the considerably greater hiring rate for women, together with previous evidence that tenure and turnover are related, one might guess that a longitudinal study would reveal that women are leaving at a less rapid rate than men, holding tenure constant.

TABLE 7.4 **Bargaining Unit Employment, Hires, and Terminations for Plants A and B Combined (1977–79 Average)**

	Women	Men
Average employment	1,898	23,290
Average terminations per year	160	1,881
Average termination rate* (per 100 employees)	8.4	8.1
Average hires per year	1,630	6,737
Average hiring rate (per 100 employees)	28.6	9.6

*Differences for women and men not statistically significant at .10 level.

Absenteeism Data

Data on absenteeism among bargaining-unit workers were available for the larger of the two study firms from 1977 and 1980. This firm reported data on two categories of absence, extended and daily. Extended absences are those occurring when employees are not scheduled to work. These absences usually reflect a known reason for inability to work in excess of one week, typically some medical problem or, in the case of women, pregnancy leaves. Daily absences, in contrast, are recorded when a worker does not show up for a scheduled shift.

Extended and daily absence data for 1977 and 1980 are summarized in Table 7.5. As reported in the table, both extended and daily absence rates were higher for women than for men in both 1977 and 1980 (significant at the .001 level). Given the limited data, we did not test for possible changes in these levels from 1977 to 1980. However, it does appear that the rate of extended absence for women has increased, possibly due to increasing use of pregnancy leaves as company policies have become more flexible on this issue.

TABLE 7.5   Extended and Daily Absence Rates for Men and Women Bargaining Unit Workers in Plant A 1977 and 1980

	1977		1980	
	Men	Women	Men	Women
(1) Total work turns available in year (number employed × 250 turns per year)	4,507,250	192,750	4,346,000	327,000
(2) Number of work turns on extended absence	97,235	8,958	87,794	22,102
(3) Proportion of work turns on extended absence: (2) ÷ (1)	.0215*	.0465*	.0202*	.0676*
(4) Total work turns scheduled: (1) − (2)	4,410,015	183,792	4,258,206	304,898
(5) Number of work turns on daily absence	148,452	6,791	106,932	10,317
(6) Proportion of work turns on daily absence: (5) ÷ (4)	.0337*	.0369*	.0251*	.0338*

*All differences in men and women absence rates are significant at the .001 level.

EVALUATING THE PERFORMANCE OF WOMEN:
THE VIEWPOINT OF MANAGEMENT

In the absence of extensive objective indices to evaluate the performance of women in the steel industry, we turn to a series of questions
asked in the interviews with supervisory personnel. As will be recalled from
Chapter 5, we systematically sampled managers at three levels of supervision: department superintendents and assistant superintendents, general
foremen, and turn foremen (first-line supervisors).

From the supervisors, we were interested in learning about possible
increased costs that they associated with the recent hiring of women. If
supervisors believed that costs had increased in one or more crucial areas,
then we might infer something about the performance of women. To this
end, we asked supervisors to evaluate the effect of women on each of the
following areas: training costs, supervision costs, maintenance costs,
absenteeism, turnover, productivity, morale, and cooperation among
workers. Their responses were assessed on 7-point scales, for which the
anchors were "greatly reduced" (1), "no effect" (4), and "greatly increased"
(7). Table 7.6 presents the frequency with which each response was
endorsed, and the mean rating for each area of concern.

As can be seen from this table, the modal response to each of our
questions was that the increased hiring of women had no effect. There is
considerable variability, however, and in many cases supervisors do
perceive greater costs. In terms of training, supervision, maintenance,
absenteeism, and turnover, supervisors perceive significant increases due to
women (i.e., the mean rating is statistically greater than the "no effect"

TABLE 7.6 Supervisor's Evaluations of the Effects of Women

	Percentage Endorsing Each Response[a]							Mean Rating
	1	2	3	4	5	6	7	
Training costs	—	—	1.0	59.6	17.3	13.5	5.8	4.6
Supervision costs	—	1.0	—	31.7	26.0	24.0	16.3	5.2
Maintenance costs	—	1.0	1.9	63.5	21.2	5.8	5.8	4.5
Productivity	5.8	8.7	29.8	42.3	7.7	3.8	—	3.5*
Absenteeism	—	1.0	4.8	40.4	18.3	17.3	15.4	4.9
Turnover	—	—	3.8	51.0	25.0	13.5	5.8	4.7
Morale	5.8	9.6	25.0	30.8	16.3	10.6	1.0	3.8*
Worker cooperation	2.9	6.7	20.2	40.4	20.2	6.7	1.0	3.9*

[a]Percentages may not add to 100 due to missing data.

*Scales reversed from others; i.e., high productivity, morale, and worker cooperation are
desirable, whereas low training, supervision and maintenance costs, absenteeism and turnover
are desirable.

position). Supervisors also see a significant decrease in productivity. Only in the case of worker morale and cooperation do the ratings not diverge significantly from the neutral position. Yet while many of the differences reach statistical significance, we should also note that the verbal label being endorsed on average is only "slightly increased."

It is also noteworthy that the views of supervisors were not totally congruent with the statistical data collected in these firms. Thus, although the turnover data indicated that male and female turnover rates were comparable, 44 percent of the supervisors interviewed believed that increased hiring of women had led to higher turnover. On the other hand, more than half of the supervisors believed that absenteeism had increased, a perception that is supported by the limited analysis that we were able to perform.

Looking further at the responses of supervisors, we analyzed the data in terms of company and level of supervision. Company could be a critical factor in this regard, because the two companies were quite different in terms of the percentage of women employed. Company B, which had begun hiring women earlier, had approximately 14 percent women in the hourly work force when we conducted the study. In contrast, Company A began its affirmative action program somewhat later and had only 7 percent women in the hourly work force at the time of the study. Quite possibly, differences in length of experience with women and in the proportion of women in the work force could result in differences in attitudes toward female workers.

Indeed, there were some differences between companies. Estimates of the cost of both training and job assignment were significantly higher for supervisors at Company B. Supervisors at this company also perceived a greater decrease in productivity as a result of women, and they viewed absenteeism and turnover as more serious problems for women.[3]

Differences as a function of level of supervision were more subtle but equally interesting. In the combined analysis, there were some tendencies, although rarely significant, for upper-level supervisors to be more negative about the effects of women than were the more immediate first-line supervisors. This trend became particularly pronounced in the analysis of a question asked of supervisors at Company A alone. There, as we noted, current female employment stood at approximately 7 percent, and we asked supervisors at that company to estimate the effects if women were to constitute 20 percent of the work force. On most of these questions, level of supervision influenced the answers. In the case of productivity, for example, average responses of the highest and lowest level supervisors differed by nearly 1.5 scale units (accounting for almost 20 percent of the variance in responses). Thus those supervisors with the greatest authority and influence were the most negative about the potential costs of an increased female work force. Conversely, those supervisors who had the most direct day-to-day experience with women workers were also the most benign about their potential effects.

In another attempt to learn what management thought about women's performance, we asked the supervisors to talk about men and women in relation to specific jobs. For example, we asked them if there were any jobs that women did better than men, and if there were any jobs that men did better than women. We also asked about jobs that women and men did equally well.

The vast majority of supervisors (88 percent) said there were jobs that men did better than women. Most often they pointed either to specific labor or specific operating jobs, and superior physical strength was the reason most often given for the presumed male superiority. At the same time, nearly the same proportion of supervisors thought men and women do equally well on at least *some* jobs. Only 12 percent were willing to say that women are equal to men on all jobs.

More than half of the supervisors also pointed to jobs that they thought women did better than men. Most often these jobs involved some form of clerical work, which supervisors felt women did better because of personality traits, special training, or innate ability. Typical of these comments is the following quotation from a production superintendent: "Women do better on clerical work. They can handle repetitious work without getting bored, and they have better handwriting than men."

Supervisors were also asked if there were certain jobs that women and men tended to prefer or to avoid. There was a fair degree of similarity in the supervisors' answers to these questions. The majority believed that there are jobs that both women and men avoid, generally particular labor jobs or particular operating jobs that have heavy physical demands. For men, dirt is thought to be the primary reason for avoiding these jobs. For women, physical demands are again invoked. In addition, supervisors—and most notably the higher-level supervisors—believe that women avoid jobs because of heat factors. Once again, there is the suggestion that the perceptions of higher-level supervisors do not always mirror the beliefs of the first-level supervisors.

There was greater similarity when supervisors were asked what kinds of jobs women and men prefer. It is apparent that there are a number of highly desirable jobs within each department, jobs with lower physical demands, more pleasant environmental conditions, and in some cases, greater autonomy. All workers seem to be aware of these jobs, and men and women do not differ—at least in the opinion of the supervisors—in their tendency to seek out these jobs whenever possible.

EVALUATING THE PERFORMANCE OF WOMEN:
THE VIEWPOINT OF MALE WORKERS

If first-level supervisors tend to be more positive (or less negative) about the performance of women than higher-level supervisors, then it becomes particularly interesting to consider the viewpoint of male workers, who have perhaps even more contact with the women. Although not every man that we interviewed had daily interaction with women, most (more than 80 percent) did, and most of these encountered several women in the course of a day. Further, the majority of women that men dealt with were doing jobs similar to those the men were doing. In other words, the men's contacts were not with the secretarial or technical personnel, but rather with laborers, operatives, and craft workers like themselves.

To determine general perceptions of the effects of women, we asked the male workers a set of questions similar to those that we had asked the supervisors. Specifically, we asked the men to estimate the effect that hiring women had had on their ability to do their own job, on the quality of work done in the department, on productivity, on general worker morale, and on the level of cooperation among workers. Their responses to these questions are shown in Table 7.7.

Once again, we find that the reactions are varied, although the modal response is that the increased hiring of women has had no effect on any of these areas. Similarly, all of the means are very close to the midpoint of "no effect." Anecdotal comments from male workers testify to the diversity of

TABLE 7.7   Male Workers' Evaluations of the Effects of Women

| | Percentage Endorsing Each Response[a] | | | | | | | Mean[b] |
	1	2	3	4	5	6	7	Rating
Worker's ability to do his own job	2.5	6.7	10.0	75.8	2.5	1.7	.8	3.8
Quality of work done in the department	1.7	6.7	14.3	67.2	7.6	2.5	—	3.8
Productivity	4.2	5.9	15.3	62.7	8.5	2.5	.8	3.8
Worker morale	5.1	7.6	17.8	45.8	15.3	8.5	—	3.8
Cooperation among workers	1.7	4.3	17.1	57.3	13.7	4.3	1.7	4.0

[a]Percentages may not add to 100 due to missing data.
[b]Scale definition: 1 = greatly reduced; 4 = no effect; 7 = greatly increased (or improved).

attitudes. One worker, for example, said he thought that bringing women into the steel mills was the best thing that could have happened, and he was convinced that women did better work than men. In contrast, another worker vehemently argued that women don't belong in the mills and that their effect could only be negative.

When asked specifically whether female workers had problems in their department, more than two-thirds of the male workers asserted that they did. Often they cited physical factors, mentioning either the physical limitations of women or the physical demands of the job. The following comments are typical.

> Some jobs aren't what women planned on—heavy lifting, breathing dust for eight hours, oil or grease.

> Women can't work in labor. Supervisors should assign them where they can do the work.

> On some jobs, changing gun locks or belts, the women can't handle it.

An equal percentage of men felt that women had problems in the steel mills generally. Again, physical components of the job were among the major reasons given. In addition, men mentioned the psychological characteristics of women, as well as negative behaviors on the part of male workers, including incidents of sexual harassment. "Women get harassed a lot," one white motor inspector told us. Another man said, "Women have trouble adjusting to the language used in an all-male environment." More succinctly, a black mechanic observed that women "have to fight off wolves. Women should learn to deal with it; that's just how guys are."

It is interesting to speculate as to why interpersonal problems were reported more frequently from the distant perspective of the mill in general than in the immediate context of the worker's own department. One possible explanation is that it is easier to acknowledge such incidents when they are removed from one's own area of involvement and responsibility. Alternatively, it may be that rumors of events in other departments may magnify their occurrence, while first hand observation in one's own department may keep estimates closer to reality.

Despite the heavy invocation of physical factors, and to a lesser extent interpersonal situations, when explaining the problems that women have, male workers made many more attributions to the woman herself when asked what contributes to a women's success in the mills. "Her attitude," was the most frequent response, mentioned by nearly half of the male workers. In elaborating on this explanation, the workers suggested that if the women had the right attitude, if she wanted to do the work, and if she didn't have a chip on her shoulder, then that women could succeed in the steel mills. Approximately 25 percent of the men gave a "bottom-line" response to this question: if women could do the job, then they would succeed. Illustrative of this viewpoint are the following quotes:

It depends on the woman.

Be here every day, and do her job right.

Her mental attitude and determination. She has to tolerate dirt, crude language, dirty pictures—something completely different from what she's used to.

At the same time, there was some suggestion that the performance of women might not always be judged in the same context as that of men. Nearly half of the men, for example, believed that supervisors do not always assign the same jobs to women as they do to men. Some of these differential assignments were trivial, for example the clean-up jobs in the women's washrooms. More often, however, the men pointed to specific labor jobs, describing jobs that required considerable physical exertion and that were believed to be beyond the capacity of women. For example, "Scarfing is very physical, with 150 pounds of pressure equipment. Some women can push it, but most don't want the physical labor, and can't take the heat."

Supervisors can exercise considerable latitude in their job assignments, giving the heaviest jobs to the strongest workers and reserving less demanding jobs for the worker who is more slight of stature, less mobile, and so forth. However, to the extent that these assignments are believed to be based not on individual criteria but rather on sex alone, then it is likely to create a problem for women in the mill and resentment on the part of their male coworkers. The following quotes illustrate this problem.

Some foremen show slight favoritism to some women. They should have no favoritism—it should be by seniority only.

Foremen are afraid they (women) can't handle the tough jobs.

EVALUATING THE PERFORMANCE OF WOMEN: THE VIEWPOINT OF FEMALE WORKERS

Our third perspective on the performance of women in steel mill jobs comes from the women themselves, whose answers to questions similar to those asked of supervisors and male workers are reported in Table 7.8. Although, as was true for other groups, the modal response was that women had had no effect in areas such as quality of work, productivity, and

TABLE 7.8   Female Workers' Evaluations of the Effects of Women

| | Percentage Endorsing Each Response[a] | | | | | | | Mean |
	1	2	3	4	5	6	7	Rating
Worker's ability to do her own job	—	4.1	4.1	75.5	7.1	5.1	4.1	4.2
Quality of work done in the department	—	2.0	7.1	62.6	14.1	11.1	3.0	4.3
Productivity	2.1	2.1	3.2	67.4	12.6	8.4	4.2	4.3
Worker morale	4.2	4.2	11.6	42.1	18.9	14.7	4.2	4.3
Cooperation among workers	4.2	2.1	13.5	43.8	17.7	12.5	6.3	4.3

[a]Percentages may not add to 100 due to missing data.

morale, the answers were generally skewed toward the positive end. On all five of these questions, women were significantly more positive than were the male workers or the supervisors. It is clear that the majority of women see the move toward hiring women as at least a neutral, and often a positive, phenomenon.

The fact that women felt that most of them were doing well does not mean that they were unaware of the existence of problems. More than half reported that women did have problems in the steel mills, although their view of the problems was somewhat different from that of their male coworkers. Only half as many women as men mentioned physical strength as being a significant problem, although the issue was raised. One woman who worked in a tool room observed, "Women have to be able to be (like) a man, that is, lift heavy things. Some women can't, and they're afraid of heights." More graphically, a female millwright helper told us that "all the lifting tears up your insides too much."

Mentioned almost equally as often by women were two other problems—difficulties with supervision and negative behavior on the part of male workers. These same problems were cited when women were asked to comment more generally on problems that females have in the mills. Typical of these perceptions were the following comments:

> I would like to see a lot more women supervisors. You can't always talk to a man foreman.

> Women have trouble getting higher jobs because men still run the steel mills.

> My biggest problem is management. My general foreman plays favorites and is a bit of a racist. (stated by a black female laborer)

Vocabulary is the problem—men have vulgar mouths. Sometimes nude pictures are all over the wall. They don't like women working, they try to embarrass you. We need more male understanding. Men need to learn that women won't just be sitting in offices. They don't want to acknowledge a woman's place is not just in the home.

A woman has to be tough, and close her ears and ignore the things that are said. She can't let her feelings be hurt.

Thus women, far more than the male workers or predominantly male supervisors, were apt to report problems with the human environment, with the people with whom they interacted in the daily course of their jobs. Such a difference in perspective is not particularly surprising. Research in the area of attribution theory has shown us that people will often explain their own behaviors by events outside of themselves, whereas observers will look to the persons themselves. Both men and women in a sense are looking elsewhere to the problems—men away from themselves and toward the women, and women away from themselves and toward the males with whom they interact. Our data certainly do not allow us to decide that one or the other group has a monopoly on truth; undoubtedly there is some validity in both positions. Yet these findings do suggest the importance of obtaining more than one perspective on the problem and underline the interdependency of interactions in a complex work setting.

Although male and female workers showed considerable divergence in their definitions of the problems that women have, there was far greater convergence in their view of the solution. Women, like men, saw the individual woman's attitude and motivation as the keys to successful performance. In fact, nearly two-thirds of the women that we interviewed saw this as the major factor, reflected in statements such as the following:

It just takes guts.

Some women feel they have to act like in Victorian days. They approach men like women, rather than as a coworker.

Determination is the key. Any woman can make it here if she wants to.

SUMMARY

Can women do the work that is required in the traditionally male steel industry? We return to this question, posed at the beginning of the chapter, much more knowledgeable but with fewer final answers than we would like to have. For the most part, objective indices of performance were lacking. We can not say with certainty whether women can lift as much, walk as fast, or learn as quickly. Ideally, we would be able to sample behavior, equating for experience on the job, and assess with some degree of accuracy whether the sexes differed in performance, either at time of hiring or after some period of training. These ideal data we do not have. Unfortunately, neither do the managements of the companies we studied.

In this research, our objective measures were limited to absenteeism and turnover data, and here the picture is mixed. Turnover figures indicate no problems with women persisting, and in fact the figures are somewhat better than might be expected, given the limited tenure of most female steelworkers. In contrast, the absenteeism data that we obtained from one company indicated rather substantial differences between women and men, with women having greater absences. These differences were significant both for daily absences and extended absences. The difference in extended absences is believed to be due to pregnancy leaves, rather than different injury rates for females. Although speculative, one reason for more frequent daily absence of women may be the woman's greater responsibility for children's illness and problems, an explanation particularly likely in view of the high proportion of single-parent mothers in our sample.

With only limited objective material on performance, we must rely mainly on the statements of supervisors, the male workers, and the female workers themselves. In only a few instances can we check these perceptions against the true state of affairs. For example, in the case of absenteeism and turnover, supervisors tended to believe that women had caused figures to increase. It appears that they were right in the case of absenteeism and wrong in the case of turnover.

In other areas, we have only expressed attitudes to rely upon. Overall, the picture is a fairly optimistic one. There is a general tendency for both supervisors and workers to think that women have had little effect on the work-related dimensions. Yet within this general picture there are some darker shadings. For example, supervisors at the company that had longer experience with women and had more women in the work force were more negative than were comparable people in the company with less experience. With only two companies in our study, it is of course dangerous to put too much stock in this difference, as the companies differed on a number of other dimensions as well. Nonetheless, it is a factor of concern that should be addressed in future research, perhaps by conducting longitudinal studies that could look at patterns in a single company over time, as well as a larger sample of companies.

It is also interesting to observe the differences that occasionally emerged as a function of level of supervision. Discrepancies between upper- and lower-level supervision were quite large in some cases. Furthermore, the fact that the least positive views of women were held by those managers who had the greatest responsibility for policy suggests a potential area of difficulty for women trying to enter the industry in increasing numbers.

Throughout our study, we encountered incidents in which women did not appear to be doing the job well and where preferential treatment was not helping the woman and was alienating the men. Yet we also encountered reports of men not doing their jobs, being lazy, goofing off, and the like. In the final analysis, questions concerning the performance of women, to the extent that we were able to answer them, were most often answered positively.

NOTES

1. This suggests, of course, that the management of the plants we studied are also unable to measure objectively the impact of women on production. We believe that this is, in fact, the case.

2. The turnover and hiring rates used are those recommended by the U.S. Department of Labor (Gleuck, 1978):

$$\frac{\text{Number of terminations (hires) during year}}{\text{Total number of employees at midyear}} \times 100$$

Because they are calculated using the same base employment, the termination rates and hiring rates may be compared directly.

3. In general, these differences were small in magnitude, averaging half a scale point or less, but they were clearly significant. Variance accounted for by the differences ranged from 2 percent to 9 percent.

8

Women in
the Steel Mill:
Self-Evaluation, Satisfaction,
and Aspirations

From consideration of women as a group and their performance in the mills, we now turn to a more individual perspective, and explore the attitudes of the women themselves. How women feel about their steel mill jobs is important. If women strongly dislike working in the mills, then no amount of public policy pressure to hire women steel workers will lead to increased employment of women in the long run.

One piece of data from the last chapter, the turnover data, suggests that women of steel like their jobs well enough to stay with them. They aren't leaving at a rate any greater than their male counterparts. Yet turnover data for a short period of time in a rather weak economy may not tell the whole story. Perhaps women view their steel mill jobs as temporary. Or perhaps they dislike them, but stay until they can accumulate some savings from their high wages.

This chapter probes the attitudes of women steel workers toward their jobs. How do their jobs fit their expectations? How do the women feel about their work and their surroundings? What are their future plans and aspirations?

SELF-EVALUATIONS
OF FEMALE STEEL WORKERS

As reported in the previous chapter, women tend to be quite positive in their evaluations of women's performance in general. Thus, when considering the effect of women as a whole, most female workers said at minimum that the increased numbers of women had had no effect. Almost as often, they indicated that women had made positive contributions to both production and interpersonal relations. Given this generally optimistic view of women as a whole, it is perhaps not surprising that women view their own individual performance in positive terms as well.

When asked in global terms, how good are you at your job, nearly 60 percent of the women we interviewed said that they were better than other workers—either somewhat better (48 percent) or much better (12 percent). Nearly 40 percent felt that they were about the same as other workers, and less than 2 percent felt that they were worse. This distribution of responses is in fact quite similar to the responses of the male workers that we interviewed, and there were no significant differences between the two groups. It is evident that in evaluating themselves in front of an unknown interviewer, almost no workers of either sex were willing to admit inferiority. Whether in more anonymous and private conditions, more personal doubts would have been evident, we do not know. However, there is no reason to think that women and men would have been different in this respect. (And in fact, if a difference were suspected, the psychological literature would predict that women would be more humble in public.)

We pursued this question in more detail by asking the workers to evaluate themselves on a set of 11 specific job-related dimensions, dealing with education and training, physical strength and endurance, and interpersonal aspects of the job. As shown in Table 8.1, the similarities between women and men are far more striking than the differences. On 9 of the 11 dimensions, there are no significant differences between the women and men. Only in the case of physical strength and endurance did women rate themselves less positively than men, and even there the differences were quite small in any absolute sense, amounting to only about .2 of a scale point. In each case, both women and men rated themselves somewhere between being the same as others and being somewhat better than others.

The similarities between women and men in self-evaluation are interesting to observe, particularly in the context of considerable laboratory research that has shown women to be more self-denigrating than men on such evaluation tasks (Deaux, 1976). Yet as more detailed analysis has shown, even in the laboratory context, sex differences are to a large degree dependent on familiarity with the task at hand (Deaux, 1977). In the present case, we can assume that men and women had equal familiarity with the job. Although their experience differed to some extent—not greatly, however, as we for the most part attempted to match women and men in terms of tenure—basic familiarity with the job could be assumed, as all of our respondents had worked in the mills for at least six months. Given a self-selected sample of males and females in a familiar environment, we are dealing with a situation in which sex differences are much less likely, and in this case, rarely found. Nevertheless, it is not inconsequential that women were as self-assured as men in this previously all-male setting.

It is also worth noting that both men and women tended to rate themselves higher in the area of interpersonal relations, particularly on those questions that asked about the attitudes of others (either supervisors or coworkers) toward themselves. Recall that these dimensions were also those considered most important by both supervisors and workers when asked what determines good performance within the steel mills. It is difficult to know if the workers' views of the general importance of various characteristics biased their own self-assessment on these dimensions, which were obtained later in the interviews. It seems quite possible that such a bias may be a natural part of the social judgment process—that all of us come to rate as more important those aspects of performance on which we ourselves excel (or at least do better than average). Whatever bias does exist is no more prominent in women than in men.

TABLE 8.1 Mean Self-Evaluations of Female and Male Workers

	Female	Male	Significance Level of Difference
Work experience	3.48	3.59	N.S.
Vocational training	3.21	3.35	N.S.
Formal education	3.36	3.29	N.S.
Physical endurance	3.42	3.63	.038
Physical strength	3.21	3.49	.008
Attitudes toward coworkers	3.64	3.72	N.S.
Ability to deal with hazing	3.65	3.84	N.S.
Attitude toward immediate supervisor	3.60	3.68	N.S.
Immediate supervisor's attitude toward worker	3.90	4.04	N.S.
Department superintendent's attitude toward worker	3.63	3.80	N.S.
Coworkers' attitudes toward worker	4.02	4.13	N.S.

Note: Ratings were made on a 5-point scale on which 1 = much worse than others, and 5 = much better than others.

WORKING IN THE MILLS:
LIKES AND DISLIKES

Entering a steel mill for the first time can be an awe-inspiring experience. For the first-time visitor, perhaps the most striking qualities are the size, the small number of workers in evidence, the noise, and, in some parts of the plant, the dirt. (In other parts of the mill, the absence of dirt is perhaps most remarkable.) The scale of equipment and machinery is much larger than most people are accustomed to seeing.

We wondered what the workers that we interviewed found most difficult to adjust to when they began working in the mills. Many of the workers may have been familiar with steel mills before, of course. As we reported in Chapter 5, the majority of both women and men had relatives who were currently working in some steel mill, and the fathers of a third of both male and female workers had also worked in the mills. Yet visitation is not the same as permanent employment. Further, in many cases there is reason to believe that women previously had less familiarity with the steel mills in particular and with heavy industry and blue-collar work in general.

Retrospective reports are not terribly reliable, we recognize. And in this case, we were testing people's memories over different periods of time—from less than 6 months in the case of the most recently hired workers to a period of 15 years or longer in the case of a few male workers. Thus although these recollections are certainly not definitive, they can be suggestive.

Among the women, there was no central theme that predominated. In percentages varying from 10 to 15, women mentioned each of the following areas: exercise and physical exertion; work schedule; working with men; and environmental factors such as dirt, noise, and temperature. Examples of some of their comments are as follows:

> The heaviness of the work—I had never picked up a shovel before.

> Putting up with the garbage guys give you and not getting your feelings hurt.

> I was scared to death the first three months. It was all men!

The male workers, in contrast, showed somewhat greater consensus in their answers, with 28 percent mentioning the schedule as most difficult to adjust to. At least two aspects of the schedule cause problems for workers. One is the hours. Even the day shift, for many people the most desirable shift, requires an early start for a 7 A.M. beginning of the workday. More bothersome for many workers is the constant rotation of shifts, working day shifts one week, evening shifts another week, and the midnight (or "graveyard") shift another week. Many workers complained about this rotation. They also complained about the fact that the rotations were often unpredictable. Sometimes a worker might find out what shift would be required the following week only a few days in advance, making any plans for outside activities difficult.

Men reported other problems in initial adjustment, although with considerably less consensus. With a frequency similar to that of women, they mentioned dirt, noise, and temperature as problems. They also, to a greater degree than women, mentioned problems with supervision. "Getting used to some of the foremen," one white male told us when we asked about initial adjustment problems. "They give you a job and then laugh in your face, and there's nothing you can do." Another man, of Dutch and Indonesian parentage, complained of being discriminated against: "I was treated like a minority with no group."

Moving from retrospective accounts to present assessments, we asked the workers what they liked best and least about their present jobs. In this respect, the most important point to be made is that most of the workers liked their jobs quite well. In fact, 70 percent of the women interviewed said that they liked their job either quite well or extremely well, a pattern that would seem to indicate considerable satisfaction among these hard-hatted pioneers.

Specific features most often mentioned by women and men as either positive or negative aspects of their jobs are shown in Table 8.2. For

TABLE 8.2   Liked and Disliked Job Characteristics Most Frequently Mentioned by Female and Male Workers (in percentages)

Most-Liked Characteristics	Females	Males
Challenge	18.4	15.3
Freedom/lack of supervision	13.6	12.1
Pay	11.7	13.7
Other job characteristics	15.5	20.2
Nothing liked	11.7	10.5
Least-Liked Characteristics	Females	Males
Dirt/noise	17.5	30.6
Supervision	8.7	8.1
Temperature	5.8	4.8
Schedule	11.7	15.3
Nothing disliked	4.9	6.5

women, the challenge of the job and its intrinsic rewards were mentioned most often as positive aspects. As one female laborer described it, "It's different from housework. I get to meet people and learn about steel." And another woman told us, "This job is challenging—it's the best job I've ever had." Other characteristics mentioned with some regularity were the freedom that a particular job allowed and the pay.

Slightly more than 10 percent of the women found nothing that they liked about their job, a percentage that is almost duplicated by the male respondents. One woman was particularly vocal in her negative feelings about the steel mill as a place to work. "I don't like anything about it," she said; "it's horrible." Neatly coifed and dressed, although coming directly off the plant floor, this former personal secretary criticized the working conditions, the type of people who work in the mills, and the union.

Although this particular woman was rather single-minded in her dislike of the steel mills, most women to whom we talked were more limiting in the negative features that they mentioned. Most often cited were environmental factors, chiefly the dirt and the noise. For the men, these factors were more frequently mentioned, thus contradicting the stereotype that women are more bothered by negative environmental conditions. For a substantially smaller percentage of the workers, supervision was seen as a major source of difficulty. Typical of these problems were the following comments:

People seem to get ahead through favoritism and nepotism, rather than hard work.

The foremen don't treat us like people—they treat us like machines.

It is interesting to observe what appear to be some shifts in the salient features of the job as women move from their recollections of initial entry to present status. Physical demands, for example, were mentioned more in the context of initial adjustment than they were in the present context. Similarly, the problems of working with men seem to lessen. Some women specifically mentioned that whereas this had been a problem initially, it no longer was, in part because the men had grown accustomed to having women around, and in part because the women themselves had grown accustomed to working with men. As one woman graphically put it, "In the beginning, men hated women being here and were real shitheads, but it's OK now."

Sexual harassment was mentioned rather infrequently by the women we interviewed as being a current problem. One possible explanation of this finding is that women were simply not prone to talk about this subject to interviewers who were not only strangers but who were seemingly linked to the company management. Although this possibility can not be ruled out entirely, there is evidence that such was not the case. First, many workers were quite liberal in their criticism of the company, of management in general and of particular foremen and supervisors. Thus our guarantees of anonymity appear to have been effective in a great number of cases, if not all. Secondly, if there was reluctance to talk about sexual harassment, one might hypothesize that such reluctance would be greater in the presence of a male interviewer than when talking to a female. However, our analysis showed that there were no differences in the frequency of discussing such topics as a function of the sex of the interviewer.

It is also possible that sexual harassment was simply not as frequent as some previous studies might have predicted. Finding a lower incidence of sexual harassment is, in fact, consistent with Walshok's (1981) description of blue-collar women. As she describes it, "In the skilled blue-collar milieu the woman worked more independently, she was a peer with most of the men, she was a member of a union that *sometimes* was a resource, and she was working in an environment which was generally more tolerant of both verbal and physical aggressiveness" (Walshok, 1981, p. 239). Thus Walshok suggests that women in the blue-collar environment have more relative power than women in many occupations, and also have more direct ways to cope with initial advances that male workers may make.

A vivid example of the use of such direct strategies is evidenced in a story provided by one of the women whom we interviewed. As this woman describes the encounter that she had with a male coworker early in her employment at the company:

> He came up and asked if I needed any money. Then he put a brand-new $100 bill in my hand. I threw it right back. "It's not enough money and you're not enough man," I told him. He's never bothered me since.

This woman, of Hispanic background and now operating mobile equipment in the mill, went on to explain her belief that it is clearly up to the woman to stop such encounters. As she told us, the woman "can stop it faster than anybody or anything else."

In contrast to the interpersonal problems with male workers that appear to decrease with time, women workers seem to become more conscious of supervisory behaviors as their tenure on the job increases. Supervision is rarely mentioned in response to queries about the positive aspects of one's job.

The negative environmental aspects become no more tolerable with time, nor do workers appear to get so habituated that they are unaware of their effect. Both women and men report this to be the most negative aspect of their jobs, increasing both its rank and its frequency from the initial adjustment reports. Mention of these environmental features varies somewhat with the area of the plant. Workers in the dirtiest coke and blast furnace departments are slightly more apt to mention the dirt than are workers at the finishing end, who encounter such conditions less frequently.

WOMEN IN THE MILLS:
JOB PREFERENCES AND ASPIRATIONS

The satisfaction described above is reflected again when women are asked what jobs they might like to have within the plants. Nearly 40 percent of the women said the job currently held was identical to their most-wanted job. Beyond that testimony to the present, the aspirations of women were diverse (see Table 8.3). Their preferences differed only slightly from those of the male workers that we interviewed. Men were more likely to indicate an interest both in supervisory positions and in craft occupations than women, although the differences were only moderate. Operator positions were equally popular with women and men. Men were less prone to mention clerical positions as a desired job slot.

To understand why these particular jobs were seen as attractive, we need to consider the reasons that workers gave for their desirability. Many different job features were mentioned, varying with the particular job selected. Among the most frequently mentioned characteristics were the challenges inherent in the job, the freedom that the job allowed, or the negative features that the job did not include, such as dirt, noise, and strenuous physical demands. Often times, too, women described their own preferences and temperament as the rationale for their choice. For

TABLE 8.3 Jobs Most Frequently Mentioned as Desirable by Males and Females (in percentages)

Job Title	Females	Males
Present job	38.5	36.1
Millwright	2.0	10.6
Motor inspector	5.2	2.5
Clerical	6.3	.8
Mobile equipment operator	5.2	5.7
Janitor	2.1	0.0
Checker/stocker	5.2	1.6
Machine operator	8.4	11.5
Labor	9.4	8.2
Foreman	7.3	13.1

example, one woman, explaining why she would like to be a foreman, said that she liked being with people. Also, she acknowledged, there was some "female chauvinism" in her that reacted to the absence of women in foreman positions.

Although many workers knew what kind of job they would like in preference to their own, nearly all could point to jobs that they wouldn't want. Workers of both sexes most often indicated the basic laboring job as one they would not want; 46 percent of the women and 57 percent of the men named this single job category. The only other job to receive any kind of consensus—and a limited one at that—was the job of foreman, considered undesirable by 12 percent of the women and 15 percent of the men. Supervisory positions appear to affect approximately equal numbers of people in a positive and a negative way. Some see the job as highly desirable, while others, generally mentioning the amount of responsibility and "hassle" as undesirable features, see it as most unappealing.

Reasons for not wanting a particular job varied and again were contingent on the particular job noted. Reasons most often given by women for not wanting a specific job were the amount of physical exertion required in the job, the absence of challenge, and the dirt and noise present in the environment.

In fact, both the environmental features and the physical demands were important in most of the workers' choices of undesirable jobs and locations. In naming a department that they would like to work in, most often workers mentioned an absence of dirt and noise as a positive feature. In noting departments in which they would not like to work, more than two-thirds of the women (and an equal proportion of the men) pointed to one of the departments at the basic end of the steelmaking process, such as the coke ovens and the blast furnaces. Virtually never was one of these departments chosen as a place where the worker would want to be, except occasionally by workers already placed there who were either satisfied with their job and/or were unfamiliar with other departments within the plant.

Our understanding of the job sequences of these women steelworkers is limited. Company records were not sufficiently detailed for us to chart the exact job sequence that a worker has followed from time of employment in the company to the present. Furthermore, the questions that we posed in the interviews, both about past employment and about future goals, were not sufficiently detailed to allow a real analysis of job progression. We can, however, make some general observations that may suggest directions for future investigation.

For the majority of women in our sample, work in the steel industry represented a fairly sharp transition from previous employment. Only a minority of these women (30 percent) had worked in blue-collar jobs before; similarly, few (13 percent) had been employed in either steel or other durable industries. As Walshok (1981) also reported in her study of craft workers, the move to a blue-collar job is often not the next step in a logical developmental sequence, but rather occurs somewhat accidentally, through chance contacts or outreach programs that are specifically seeking women.

When hired by the steel companies, women are generally assigned to a particular job (most often, but not always, labor) and a particular department, depending on the needs of the company rather than the preferences or inclinations of the woman. In some cases, entrance even to craft occupations is rather accidental, as the company seeks to fill a program geared to increase the representation of women. (We will discuss these programs in more detail in Chapter 9.)

Once positioned in a specific job, change is determined by a combination of factors. One factor is the worker's willingness to bid on particular openings. Job availability is announced, or "posted," throughout the plant and workers may apply for these available positions. Here, however, seniority becomes an important determinant in the final selection. Seniority clauses have been superceded by the Consent Decree in many companies (including Company B in our study) to allow women to enter craft occupations more quickly, but seniority still plays a major role in deciding who gets what job in noncraft occupations.

Whereas special efforts have been made to open the craft jobs to women, other more prestigious (and higher-paying) jobs within the mills are still difficult for women to enter. Consider foreman positions. As we have seen, only a small percentage of women indicated this as a job they would want. Yet these aspirations may in part by shaped by the availability of models—women who do hold foreman jobs—and by the perceived likelihood that a woman could hold that position. Indeed, one personnel executive in our study expressed surprise that as many as 7 percent of women wanted supervisory work, commenting that the company has had trouble getting women interested in such jobs.

The number of women in supervisory positions is certainly quite small at present. In our sample of 104 supervisors, only 2 were women. More generally, as noted in Chapter 6, only 2.8 percent of the 3021 exempt (management) personnel at Company A were female. This number includes professional as well as managerial staff, but shows the paucity of female supervisors generally.

Comments made by some of the workers that we interviewed suggested that they do not believe these low numbers to be accidental. One white woman, currently working as a door machine operator, observed as follows: "In order to move up in the progression, you must be trained by people above you. Most men don't want to train women to move up."

And a Hispanic woman doing labor work commented, "Women supervisors don't exist here. They should give women the opportunity to become foremen." Yet not all men are opposed to women moving into supervision. One black male, himself at the subforeman level, told us, "I'd like to see more women in supervision. There are a lot of women who can do it." And a general foreman in the electrical department, who also favored an increase in women, acknowledged, "I think a woman could do my job."

Yet if women are to move into these kinds of jobs, more than their expectations have to change. Foreman appointments are usually preceded by some experience with subforeman responsibilities; these in turn are usually preceded by occasional calls to fill in on a temporary basis for a subforeman who is absent for a day or two. At present, it appears to be rare for women to be asked to fill in at this level. In part, this may be because women typically have less seniority and so are lower in the pecking order. In addition, there may still be reluctance to give women leadership functions over predominantly male work groups, or perhaps even to train them in advanced skills, as one of our respondents claimed.

One woman's story illustrates what can happen to the woman who is hired in a supervisory position, in this case directly after graduating with a degree in engineering. Although most newly hired supervisors begin with an initial placement in the office, becoming familiar with procedures and routines, this office stint is generally limited to 3 to 6 months after which the person goes out onto the floor and the actual production line. In this woman's case, she was still in the office after a year and a half, straightening files, taking notes at meetings, and getting coffee for the higher-level supervisors—in her estimation, doing many things that males hired at the same level would not be asked to do. Finally, after persistent requests, she was assigned to the floor. Yet this move came much later, she believes, than it did for comparable men for whom such a transfer would be given automatically, without repeated requests and enforced time in the office.

We do not know if this particular story is typical. Yet it is clear that few women are in supervisory positions in the steel industry, and almost none are above the stage of first-level foreman. Construction of career development sequences and programs for women within this industry may be a topic that should be given high priority by industry management and public policymakers.

THE CASE OF JANITORIAL WOMEN

In Chapter 5 we noted than an unusually high proportion of the women that we interviewed were doing janitorial work—nearly 20 percent of the women, as compared to only 1 or 2 percent of the men. It is difficult to know if this proportion is representative, as janitorial jobs are classified simply as general labor in the company's records. Nonetheless, we decided to look more closely at this particular group of women, who were essentially doing traditionally female work within the nontraditional setting of a steel plant.

The demands of a janitorial job are considerably different, and generally much less physically taxing, than many of the other jobs in the steel mills. In terms of physical activities, the major action reported by janitors is sweeping, an activity in which almost no other workers engage. In contrast, lifting, reported as a common activity by the majority of other women, was a much smaller part of the janitorial woman's activities. In terms of actual physical weight lifted, almost none of the janitorial women reported lifting anything heavier than 50 pounds, and nearly half reported lifting nothing heavier than 25 pounds. In view of these differences, it is not surprising that janitorial women report that their jobs are easier than those of other people, and that the amount of strength required is less. Because the demands of this job are so different, it becomes particularly important to consider this sample of women if we are to understand women's potential for development and advancement within the steel mill setting.

There are at least two general lines of argument that one can pursue in attempting to explain the concentration of women in janitorial positions. One is that women—either women in general, or certain kinds of women— seek out these easier and more traditional positions, vying to get in and reluctant to leave. An alternative explanation is that women are more readily assigned to these positions, independent of their own predilections, with such assignments following naturally from the set of stereotypes and beliefs that supervisors have about the abilities and the usefulness of women in the steel industry.

In attempting to sort out the evidence for these two forms of explanation, let us first look at the characteristics of the janitorial women themselves. An initial look suggests that it may not be women in general who are janitors but rather a particular subsample, as there are some notable differences between janitorial women and their nonjanitorial peers.

Ethnically, the breakdown of janitorial women fell in neat thirds: one-third black, one-third white, and one-third Hispanic. The evenness of this split, however, does not match the distribution of the women in the plants as a whole. Indeed, if we look only at the women who are *not* in janitorial jobs, we find a very different distribution: 37 percent black, 57 percent white, and only 6 percent Hispanic. As these numbers indicate, the divergence in this distribution is particularly marked for the white and Hispanic women. White women are much less likely to be in janitorial jobs, and Hispanic women are considerably more likely to be in such jobs.

Women holding janitorial jobs are also, on the average, older. The median age of these women is 37, compared to 27 years for the women holding other jobs within the companies. In some other respects, the two groups are the same. The average length of time with the company and in the department are the same (approximately two years), and women in both groups have, on the average, completed high school. Approximately the same percentage of each group of women reported being the sole wage earners in their family (61 percent and 64 percent). More of the janitorial women reported having dependents (81 percent versus 64 percent), consistent with their older average age.

The presence of dependents could be one reason why women would seek out janitorial jobs, as these jobs tend to be straight day-shift jobs. Raising children on a rotating or night-shift schedule could certainly pose problems. More janitorial women do in fact mention the schedule as the thing that they like best about their job: 9 percent versus fewer than 3 percent of the other women. Yet clearly that percentage is not very great, nor is the difference in the proportion of women having dependents large enough that this fact alone can account for the preponderance of women in janitorial positions.

There are some other differences between janitorial and nonjanitorial women in their aspirations and self-evaluations. Janitorial women evaluate their job performance more positively. On some work dimensions, there are also differences, as in the case of endurance, where female janitors rate themselves higher than do women holding other kinds of jobs. Janitorial women also feel that they have a more positive attitude toward their supervisor, yet they are less certain that the attitudes of coworkers toward them are positive. This latter finding may in part reflect the fact that people who do janitorial jobs have less frequent interaction with their coworkers. The majority of janitors (68 percent) report that they do their work alone, as compared to only 28 percent of the women holding other kinds of jobs. It is also possible that janitors *are* liked less by their coworkers. Engaged in a less demanding job but receiving the same pay, these women may be seen as getting a "free ride" and as not part of the "team."

Comparing the self-evaluations of janitors and nonjanitors is also somewhat risky because the comparison group is uncertain. These self-evaluation questions asked the workers to judge themselves in comparison to other workers. Given the fact that janitors tend not to work directly with other people and that their job is quite different from those of other workers, there seems to be a good possibility that they may have been comparing themselves primarily to other (female) janitors. For the nonjanitorial women, in contrast, it seems most likely that they used all other workers as a comparison because of their ready availability in their day-to-day activities.

At the same time, both groups of women seemed equally satisfied with their present job. An equal proportion indicated that the job they would like the most was the one they presently held (38 percent), and their overall reported liking for the jobs did not differ significantly, with the typical answer for both groups being that they liked their job quite a bit. Although both janitors and nonjanitors liked their present job to equal degrees, there were differences in the jobs that they would aspire to. Janitorial women were most likely to mention either clerical jobs or some specific labor job (typically one similar to their own and generally not representative of labor jobs). Neither of these jobs were mentioned often by nonjanitorial women, whose choices varied among craft, operative, and supervisory jobs. For example, 9 percent of the nonjanitorial women mentioned a mechanical or electrical craft job, while not a single janitorial woman did.

The reasons given for particular choices also differed substantially between the two groups. Nonjanitorial women were most likely to refer to their own interests, abilities, and traits, or to less tangible qualities of the job, such as the challenge, the accomplishment, or the ability to work on one's own without supervision. Janitors, in contrast, were most likely to mention the pay or other concrete characteristics of the job.

Not surprisingly, descriptions of their present job differ even more sharply between the two groups (see Table 8.4). When asked what they liked best about their present job, the women janitors often mentioned aspects of social interaction. For example, one janitor told us, "I enjoy myself with the people in the office. I feel like I'm part of the family." Another said, "I like to work with men and people around"; yet another talked about "getting around and seeing other people." Few women in nonjanitorial jobs referred to social interaction when asked to describe the positive features of their job. Most common were references to the challenge of the jobs and what could be learned, a quality mentioned much less frequently by the janitors.

Disliked qualities of their present jobs also differed (see Table 8.4). The most common complaint of nonjanitorial women was the dirt and noise, environmental qualities that janitorial women for the most part do not experience. Nonjanitorial women were also more likely to cite problems with supervision. Not only did the janitorial women not report this as a problem, but, in fact, more than 25 percent of these women could think of nothing negative about their present job. Some differences are also noticeable when the women described what adjustment was most difficult when first coming to the mill. Although many of the responses were the same, it is interesting to note that all complaints dealing with working with men were found among the nonjanitorial women—not a surprising outcome since the janitorial women primarily work alone or with other women.

TABLE 8.4a Job Characteristics Liked Best by Janitorial and Nonjanitorial Women

	NonJanitorial	Janitorial
Pay	12.3	9.1
Schedule	2.5	9.1
Exercise and physical demands	6.2	4.5
Work load	3.7	4.5
Freedom and lack of supervision	13.6	13.6
Challenge	21.0	9.1
Interaction	4.9	18.2

TABLE 8.4b Job Characteristics Liked Least by Janitorial and Nonjanitorial Women

	Nonjanitorial	Janitorial
Schedule	4.9	4.5
Exercise	7.4	—
Temperature	6.2	4.5
Dirt and noise	21.0	4.5
Supervision and policy	11.1	—
Interaction	4.9	9.1
Nothing	7.4	27.3

Perhaps this relative isolation from the ongoing work on the plant floor can also account for the finding that janitorial women are far less likely to say that women have problems either in their own department or in the mill in general. The percentage reporting problems in the department, for example, is nearly twice as great among the nonjanitorial women. The nature of perceived problems tends to differ as well. Whereas the janitors who do see problems report them primarily in terms of the physical strength issue, nonjanitorial women report a more diversified set of problems, including difficulties with supervision and policy, and negative attitudes, behaviors, and harassment from men. (It is interesting to note that these perceptual differences are less when the target is the mill in general, suggesting that general rumors and information networks may be more consistent than the personal experiences of the two groups of workers; or, perhaps, that there are real occupational differences and reasonably objective perceptions of the mill in general.)

Thus there are numerous differences between women who are janitors and women who are not, despite some areas of overlap. Some of these differences in response may be attributable to the job characteristics themselves. Recall that in Chapter 2 we discussed the question of job satisfaction, noting the research that has attempted to compare men and women in terms of job-related or climate-related factors of satisfaction. There we noted that the job itself could often be implicated in the analysis, suggesting that people will report being satisfied with those characteristics that are available to them or which they can reasonably expect to have within a particular job setting. In the present instance, we are comparing not women and men, but rather two groups of women—two groups who are engaged in quite different jobs, albeit within the common setting of a large integrated steel plant.

Thus one can question whether the differences that we observe are solely the result of different types of jobs, or whether we are dealing with different subgroups of women as well as different kinds of jobs. Some of the demographic differences between the groups would suggest that the former explanation may have some merit. Certain kinds of women do seem more likely to engage in janitorial jobs, although the predictors are far from perfect. Yet even if we accept this difference, a question still remains as to how these particular kinds of women arrived in these particular jobs. Although some women may well prefer janitorial work, there is a possible influence from the supervisory level as well. Some supervisors clearly think that this is an appropriate place for women to be. As one supervisor (referring to women in general) told us, "They know all about it. If you put them on a broom and leave them alone, they're happy." Yet janitorial jobs were not ones that a majority of supervisors cited as being done better by women than men. Clerical work was a far more frequent response to this question, although that too is clearly consistent with general stereotypes about women's capabilities.

In fact, we can not say with certainty to what degree stereotypic expectations on the part of supervisors lead to the assignment of women to janitorial positions. We do know, however, that women do not prefer these positions to all others, contrary to what some early statements by management had led us to believe. For example, one black woman described her janitorial job in the following terms: "It's not fulfilling. Anyone can do it—it doesn't take any intelligence. I would like something that would be more challenging." Not all women felt like that, to be sure. Yet only 38 percent of the women in janitorial jobs said that was the job they would like to have most, exactly the same proportion preferring their present job among nonjanitorial women.

From the information we have gathered, it would appear that there are some women who seek out janitorial jobs and who are perfectly content in those positions. It also seems likely that biased assumptions may lead some supervisors to assign women—and particularly minority women—to these positions, whether or not the women prefer to be janitors.

There is another aspect of this situation that may serve to perpetuate some of these choices, leading to the belief that all women who are in these positions want to stay in them. Once in a janitorial position, the worker (be it male or female) is largely out of the flow of the work situation. Removed from the floor and central production, a janitor can easily be ignored. The position can be a dead end, providing few opportunities for learning new skills or for interacting with workers and supervisors. Janitors may tend to remain janitors, not necessarily as a result of their own desires but as an inevitable consequence of being "away from the action." Just as some management positions rarely lead to the executive suite, so certain labor positions may rarely lead to the more desirable and/or higher-paying operative and supervisory positions. Thus once again we are reminded, as in the case of supervision, that entry of women into the steel mills does not guarantee their movement up the ladder.

SUMMARY

Having entered the steel mills with hard hats on head, what have the women found? Our interviews suggest that many women have found a good job that they enjoy. There are some possible qualifications to this statement. First, we interviewed only those women who have stayed with the job—who have made it through the probationary period and who were currently employed in the mills, employed on the average for two years. (However, the turnover data suggest that women and men are equally likely to stay with the job.) Second, we did interview some women who did not like their jobs. Either they did not like the particular job they had or, more broadly, they did not like anything about the steel mills (except, presumably, the pay, which justified their staying despite their negative attitudes). Again, however, the men that we interviewed were equally likely to display such negative feelings.

Yet for the most part, the women that we interviewed were satisfied with their job, often finding it a source of challenge and a marked improvement over previous jobs that they had held. Furthermore, the women that we interviewed were rather confident in their self-assessments. Although laboratory research often finds women underestimating their performance relative to men, these steel women regarded themselves on a par with men on most dimensions that we assessed. Only in the areas of physical strength and endurance did they acknowledge somewhat less ability, and even here the difference was small. Thus women not only appreciate the job, but in most cases feel that they can do it quite well.

Adjusting to the mill and the male environment has not been without problems for many of the women that we interviewed. In some cases, sexual harassment has occurred, although our findings suggest that the frequency of such harassment has not been terribly high. On the one hand, it is possible that we have underestimated the incidence because our questionnaire contained no direct inquiries about sexual harassment, and we could gauge the frequency only from open-ended answers to general questions about problems that women have. On the other hand, Walshok (1981) has also reported relatively low rates of sexual harassment in blue-collar settings, suggesting that the present results may be veridical.

There are other adjustment problems as well. Some of these problems are common to all workers, whether they be male or female. Environmental conditions such as heat, dirt, and noise are often unpleasant, and shift work that requires constant changes in schedule is difficult for all workers. Other problems are more unique to women. Working with men who are not accustomed to working with women may cause problems, either because of negative attitudes and behaviors directed toward women intentionally, or by less intentional patterns of language and behavior that were taken for granted in the all-male group. Women may also have a problem in developing a working relationship with both coworkers and supervisors—in defining their role as a worker, rather than a women who must be challenged repeatedly or assisted extensively.

Entry of women into blue-collar jobs is not the only issue. Our findings suggest that the movement of women into the sequences and up through the ranks may still be impeded. We found very few women supervisors, and attitudes expressed by some men suggest that women in such positions would not be universally accepted. Similarly, although our data are sketchy, it appears that women are not always receiving the opportunities to acquire skills that would enable them to assume foreman positions, for example by serving as subforeman on a fill-in and occasional basis.

There is also evidence that women are overconcentrated in certain dead-end positions, most notably the janitorial job. This concentration does not appear to be simply or even primarily the result of discriminatory assignment, but results in part from the predilections of some of the women themselves. To the extent that differential assignment exaggerates this trend, it serves as another impediment to women's development and advancement.

In other cases, women are moving up in the ranks. Craft workers, whom we will describe in the next chapter, represent a group of women who are moving to the more prestigious and better-paying, skilled positions. Our interviews suggest that there are more women who wish to follow this lead, both into the crafts and into supervisory positions as well. In summary, and at the risk of oversimplifying a more complex picture, these women of steel want to stay.

9

Women in
the Steel Mill:
The Craft Occupations

Craft jobs are generally among the highest-paid and have traditionally been the most prestigious of blue-collar occupations. At the same time, they have tended to be the most demographically homogeneous of blue-collar jobs—neither women nor minorities have been very visible among their ranks. As we noted earlier, the consent decree in the steel industry directed specific attention to the crafts and formulated specific provisions concerning the entrance of women into this primarily male domain.

In this chapter, we look at this group of steel women, who are either in the process of apprenticeship training or who have completed a program and are full-fledged craft workers (journeymen). These women are truly a minority within a minority. In 1979, for example, only 2.2 percent of the craft workers in these two companies were women—a total of 197 women as compared to 8,583 men in comparable positions. For these women, we would anticipate that the demands would be highest and the pressures the greatest.

Before turning to the particulars of these steel industry women, however, it will be useful to look more closely at the general position of craft

Portions of this chapter were reported earlier in J.C. Ullman and K. K. Deaux, "Recent efforts to increase female participation in apprenticeship in the basic steel industry in the Midwest," in V.M. Briggs, Jr. & F.F. Foltman (eds.), *Apprenticeship research: Emerging findings and future trends*. Ithaca, N.Y.: New York State School of Industrial and Labor Relations, Cornell University, 1981.

occupations, within American industry generally and within the steel industry specifically. We will also consider in some detail the entry routes for women into craft occupations, with an emphasis on the unique recruitment and training programs developed in the companies that we studied.

CRAFT OCCUPATIONS IN THE UNITED STATES

The U.S. Department of Labor recognizes some 400 craft occupations or skilled trades (U.S. Department of Labor, 1976). Crafts are those blue-collar occupations requiring a lengthy training period, varying from one to six years, usually achieved through an apprentice program. Because of advancing technology and the associated need to build and maintain ever-larger amounts of increasingly sophisticated equipment in industry, craft workers represent an increasing proportion of blue-collar workers. In 1980 there were 12.5 million employed craft workers in the United States, accounting for 40 percent of the 30.8 million blue-collar workers (Bureau of Labor Statistics, 1981). By way of comparison, in 1958 there were 8.5 million craft workers in the U.S., representing 20 percent of total blue-collar workers (Bureau of Labor Statistics, 1973). Thus the craft proportion of the blue-collar work force has doubled in just over two decades. Table 9.1 shows employment in the largest craft groups in 1958 and 1980.

The largest individual crafts in 1980 were automobile mechanics (1,197,000), carpenters (1,185,000), heavy equipment mechanics (963,000),

TABLE 9.1 Employment in Major Craft Groups in 1958 and 1980

	1958		1980	
	Number (×10³)	% of total	Number (×10³)	% of total
Carpenters	837	10.0	1185	9.5
Construction crafts, other than carpenters	1593	19.0	2503	20.0
Mechanics and repairmen	2070	24.6	3320	26.5
Metal craft workers	1037	12.3	638	5.1
Foreman, n.e.c.	1152	13.7	1729	13.8
All other	1715	20.4	3154	25.2
Total	8404	100.0	12,529	100.1

Sources: Bureau of Labor Statistics, April 1981; and Bureau of Labor Statistics, 1973.

electricians (648,000), and machinists (567,000). No other craft had as many as half a million workers (Bureau of Labor Statistics, 1982).

Although most people associate craft workers with the construction industry, in 1980 only 27 percent (3,322,000) of all U.S. craft workers were in cosntruction. The largest number (4,209,000, constituting 34 percent) were in manufacturing (Bureau of Labor Statistics, 1981). This concentration of craft workers in manufacturing has been true for a number of years. In both 1958 and in 1980, 19 percent of manufacturing workers were in crafts.

Women historically have played a very minor role in craft employment in the United States. In 1958 only 234,000 women were craft workers, representing 3 percent of the total craft work force (Bureau of Labor Statistics, 1973). By 1974, women's share of craft jobs had reached 4 percent, and by 1980 the figure was 6 percent (Bureau of Labor Statistics, 1975, 1981). Thus, although the female share of total craft employment has doubled over the past two decades, women still hold only a trivial proportion of craft jobs. Further, women are concentrated in a few crafts, such as beauticians and bakers. Fewer than 2 percent of carpenters, electricians, auto mechanics, pipefitters, or heavy equipment mechanics were women in 1980 (Bureau of Labor Statistics, 1981).

APPRENTICESHIP AS A MEANS OF TRAINING CRAFT WORKERS

The institution of apprenticeship dates back to ancient Babylonia and the Code of Hammurabi some 4,000 years ago. Apprenticeship was also widespread in ancient Greece, Rome, Egypt and India (Koeible, 1954). In these societies, an artisan would adopt a young boy for the purpose of teaching him a craft. After completing his training, the boy was returned to his family and expected to practice his trade. Girls were excluded from this practice, thus providing a historical precedent for more modern statistics.

Turning to modern times, one finds little interest in apprenticeship training in the United States until the beginning of World War I (Koeible, 1954). Until that time, immigrants who had been trained in Europe provided sufficient numbers of craft workers to meet the needs. However, the combination of restricted immigration and increased wartime needs made the training of craft workers essential.

The first law encouraging and regulating apprentice training was passed by Wisconsin in 1911. This law "provided for legal indenturing of apprentices with stipulated working hours in the several basic skills required in a particular trade, the hours of instruction in related subjects and the wages, which increased at regular intervals" (Koeible, 1954, p. 9). In

1937, the federal government enacted the Fritzgerald Act, which called for aid in the promotion of apprenticeship programs throughout the country (Koeible, 1954).

Currently, the U.S. Department of Labor Bureau of Apprenticeship and Training and such state agencies as the Wisconsin Industrial Commission maintain apprentice program standards. The Bureau of Apprenticeship and Training (BAT) is a federal body providing assistance and information concerning establishment of apprentice programs and maintenance of standards. The Bureau also works with state and other federal agencies to promote the welfare of apprenticeship generally. State agencies perform functions similar to those of BAT, and also administer state laws regulating apprenticeship programs.

Several common standards cover apprenticeship programs in the United States (Kunsh, 1958, p. 91):

1. A minimum age of 16.
2. A specific work schedule to be followed, showing the experience the apprentice can expect to receive and the wage schedule.
3. Instruction in related subjects.
4. Adequate supervision and appropriate records.
5. Employer-employee joint efforts to establish a program.
6. Proper ratio of apprentices employed to community needs.

The heart of apprenticeships is on-the-job training. The typical pattern is the "learn as you work" method of training. Training in this sense may mean anything from acquisition of fundamental skills to a "process of learning slightly new techniques, and modifications of old skills to fit specific company labor requirements and of practicing these new tasks in production until maximum efficiency and full wage scales are attained" (Perlman, 1969, p. 66). Apprenticeship also includes related classroom training in skills not readily learnable on the job. For example, instruction in mechanical drawing and basic mathematics may be included in a classroom segment.

Most apprenticeship programs are conducted cooperatively by unions and employers. In many areas, local labor-management apprenticeship committees oversee the program. There are approximately 9,000 of these joint apprenticeship committees in the United States, and their functions include selection of applicants, supervision of training, and certification of those people who complete their full term of indenture (U.S. Department of Labor, 1976).

As with craft jobs generally, women have not fared well in getting into apprenticeship programs. In June 1978, women constituted only 2.6 percent of all apprentices currently in training (Employment and Training

Administration, 1979). In construction crafts, where programs to combat racial discrimination have been active for a decade or more, women are even less in evidence. At the close of 1978, women held only 1.9 percent of apprenticeship openings, despite considerable publicity concerning their entrance into this field (Labor Letter, *Wall Street Journal*, 1980).

Academic concerns about the paucity of women in apprenticeable occupations is a remarkably recent phenomenon. A 1976 text by three leading employment and training scholars devotes two full pages of a chapter on apprenticeship to decrying the small number of blacks in the field and to racial discrimination. There is no reference at all to the small number of women in apprenticeable occupations. The authors' inattention to the lack of women is most evident in their statement that "the traditional father-son relationship in many skilled crafts is weakening because it discriminated against minorities and because many craftsmen with higher incomes send their sons to college" (Levitan et al., 1976, p. 211).

As the above discussion reveals, female participation in formal apprentice programs is considerably less than their proportion of craft jobs. It is enlightening to consider the reasons for this discrepancy. First, it should be noted that not all craft workers go through an apprenticeship. Indeed, in many occupations most workers obtain the skills of their trade in other ways. Some of these alternative routes include (a) completing only part of an apprenticeship; (b) picking the trade up on the job or in the armed forces; and (c) working in nonunion jobs, and then transferring into unionized programs during organizing campaigns or during periods of full employment of union craftsmen (Levitan et al., 1981).

Because entry into apprenticeship has historically been passed from father to son or nephew, women have generally been excluded from referrals. Entry through other channels into the crafts have been more feasible for women due to the absence of a need for formal approval by the journeymen. As we shall see, women steel workers have also found nonapprentice and nontraditional routes into the crafts more available.

CRAFT WORKER COMPENSATION

It was noted at the beginning of this chapter that craft jobs traditionally have been among the highest-paid blue-collar occupations. To put this assertion in perspective, two points should be made. First, no craft occupation appears on the list of the ten occupations with the highest median weekly earnings in 1981 for either men or women (Bureau of Labor Statistics, March 1982). Male craft and kindred workers in this survey reported average weekly earnings of $360, compared with $507 for civil engineers, the occupation ranking tenth among males. Women craft workers earned an average of $239 weekly, compared to the $318 per week earned by the tenth-ranked female occupation of librarians. Thus although craft workers are well paid in comparison with blue-collar workers generally, they earn far less than workers in many white-collar occupations.

The second point is related to the first. There is a common perception that electricians, plumbers, and other construction craft workers are better paid than many professionals. This perception is based on the high hourly rates negotiated by union construction workers in some areas in recent years. However, very few construction workers work a full year, due to weather constraints on outdoor work. Furthermore, only a minority of construction workers are currently unionized, and nonunion craft workers in construction earn far less per hour than do their unionized counterparts.

Earnings of craft workers do not exceed those of other blue-collar workers to the extent that one might imagine, even though they are, on the average, higher. According to the 1981 Department of Labor Survey, machine operators earn on the average $298 per week if they are male and $187 per week if they are female. These earnings are about 20 percent less than the average earnings of male and female craft workers. Given the training required of craft workers, these differences seem small. A comparison of earnings within particular occupations reinforces the point that craft jobs are not always the most highly paid. For example, male painters, auto mechanics, and bakers all earn less than $298 per week, the average for male machine operators. (There were not sufficient women in these particular crafts to permit a similar comparison for women.)

All of this is not to say that craft jobs are undesirable. They are generally considered prestigious, and weekly earnings in some crafts are superior. For example, among the highest-paying craft occupations are aircraft mechanics (average wages of $427 per week), electricians ($419), millwrights ($443), and structural metal workers ($455).

CRAFT OCCUPATIONS
IN THE BASIC STEEL INDUSTRY

Craft workers have an even more significant role in basic steel manufacturing than in manufacturing generally. In 1979, for example, 26.6 percent of the work force in our study mills were in craft occupations, compared to a nationwide average of 19.3 percent in all manufacturing. Further, the relative importance of craft workers has increased steadily during the past two or three decades, due to advancing technology in the steel industry. This trend is expected to continue.

Until recently, the steel industry had no standard industry-wide training program. Thus both occupational content and apprenticeship content vary among firms. One obvious consequence of this variation is restricted mobility of craft workers among firms. Under the 1968 Basic Steel Collective Bargaining Agreement, steps toward standardization were taken. The industry and the United Steelworkers of America agreed to embark on a program to standardize apprenticeship programs within the industry. As new apprentice training programs for each craft are developed, they will replace existing programs. As of May 1979, however, only two of these standardized programs had been formulated. Consequently, there were still numerous differences between plants in general, and between our two plants in particular, at the time of the study.

CRAFT EMPLOYMENT
IN THE STUDY MILLS

As indicated earlier, employment of women in craft jobs in the two plants studied remained very small in 1979, although it had improved since 1976 (see Table 6.4). Even with the affirmative action pressures and the special programs to be described, female craft employment stood at 2.2 percent. Although this figure is comparable to that in the more male-dominated crafts nationally, it is well below the 5–6 percent female share of all craft jobs.

Despite these numbers, we were relatively sanguine about the prospects for further increases in the proportion of female craft workers in these mills at the time of the study. By the end of 1979, considerable momentum seemed to have been established. Unfortunately, steel employment dropped sharply in the three years since the study. In the face of such declining employment, it is not possible to significantly improve the female share of jobs. It seems quite likely that the number of women in craft jobs has declined in these plants since 1979, as has the number of females employed in steel jobs generally (see Chapter 6). These results show the crucial role of hiring conditions on the ability of firms to implement public policy mandates, especially in occupations with lengthy training period requirements.

To move into craft jobs in the plants that were studied, workers must bid and compete with other workers, as required by the collective bargaining agreement. Workers may bid on any opening, and the most senior qualified worker who bids for the job is given the position. Thus entry into the crafts is strongly affected by length of service. Applicants from outside may be brought directly into craft openings only if there are not enough qualified bidders within the plant to fill the openings. As will be seen, however, certain types of programs may short-circuit some of these requirements, with the result that women and minorities may more easily gain access to craft tracks. For example, the steel industry consent decree, under which one of our study plants operated, required that 50 percent of craft openings be filled by a woman or a member of a racial minority.

Within the steel plants that we studied, 21 different crafts were represented. Some of these, such as pattern makers and scale makers, were numerically quite small, with fewer than ten workers within the mill engaged in that work. At the other end of the spectrum, the combination of millwrights, motor inspectors, and vocational mechanics accounted for more than half of all craft workers in these mills. These latter groups were the focus of our attention.

Motor inspectors are concerned with all of the electrical equipment in the mills. They inspect, repair, replace, install, adjust, and maintain all types of electrical equipment, and are generally responsible for keeping the electrical operations in peak condition. As one example, a typical task for a motor inspector is to make conduits and to wire the installations; another example is troubleshooting the control panels of electronic cranes.

Whereas the focus of motor inspectors is on the electrical element, millwrights and vocational mechanics deal with the mechanical components. A typical task of a millwright might be to replace rolls in the rolling mills, or to assemble and align gears, bearings, and shafts. The vocational mechanic's job is defined somewhat more broadly than that of the millwright, but the basic focus on mechanical operations is the same.

Apart from the difference in focus, many of the people we interviewed believed that the demands of the two crafts are different, with the mechanical crafts calling for greater physical capability than the electrical crafts. Consequently, it was often stated that women would do better in the latter than in the former. For example, an assistant superintendent of the electrical department in one plant said that he sees "absolutely no problem with women in electrical maintenance." This view was supported articulately by an electrical foreman who observed:

> A woman motor inspector should do as well as a man. It's not the physical or mental requirements, but what was put in her mind during her growing up years that matters.

In contrast to these benign views, the mechanical superintendent of one company noted, "the mechanical department has more varied jobs than electrical, so there are more problems. There are more dirty and physical jobs." A general foreman said, "I can easily take care of the two women I have. But if I had fifty women, I would have a terrible problem because there are so many physical jobs." Similarly, a mechanical turn foreman noted that "this is a big heavy mill. I try to treat people equally, but I can't give the women the heavy jobs, and that causes problems."

As noted in Chapter 7, an absence of actual performance data makes it difficult to evaluate these claims. In support of these perceptions, there were a somewhat greater number of women who expressed interest in electrical as opposed to mechanical crafts (see Chapter 8).

ATTITUDES OF CRAFT WORKERS

Craft workers in general tend to have somewhat different attitudes about their work than do other steel workers, generally being more positive about their jobs. Significantly more craft workers reported that the job they would most like to have was the one they currently had, and no craft workers said their own jobs were ones they would not like (versus 11 percent of the noncraft workers who had said that). Their jobs were in many respects more physical than other jobs; they reported significantly more lifting and climbing than other workers, for example. Yet it was their perception of the challenge of the job that appeared to most strongly differentiate them from other workers. Nearly one-third of the craft workers mentioned the challenge or the intrinsic satisfaction of their jobs as the most desirable feature, significantly more than other workers.

There were also differences in what they considered important to their jobs. Craft workers believed that work experience, vocational training, and formal education were all more important for doing the job well than did the noncraft workers, a perception that is probably veridical. Greater importance was also attached to a person's ability to deal with hazing, suggesting that the informal entrance requirements for this "fraternity" may be strong. In fact, a number of the responses of craft workers suggest a strong sense of identity among members of this group, a situation that may mean greater difficulty for the newcomer, and especially the woman.

It was also the case that craft workers (both men and women) saw more difficulty for women entering the mill in general, and their departments in particular. Nearly 80 percent of the craft workers alluded to some problems, compared with only 53 percent of the noncraft workers.

Although it would be of interest to compare male and female craft workers on a variety of evaluative dimensions, such comparisons are not feasible. Of the women we interviewed in craft jobs, more than two-thirds were still in some stage of apprentice training. In contrast, nearly two-thirds of the men were already full-fledged journeymen craft workers. Thus the two groups of craft workers, taken in their totality, are not really comparable, and equivalent subsets are too small numerically to warrant statistical analysis. Again we see how recent the entrance of women into the crafts has been.

RECRUITMENT AND TRAINING PROGRAMS
FOR WOMEN

Craft jobs in industrial settings have certainly not been a traditional goal of women. Until recently, most vocational training programs in schools emphasized quite different skills for boys and girls, offering shop classes to the former and home economics to the latter. Similarly, high school counselors have often guided boys and girls in different directions. Parents may also emphasize these differences, teaching their sons to work on cars and repair lawn mowers while showing their daughters how to cook meals and darn socks. Whatever the forces that have predominated, there is little question that, on the average, males and females arrive at the employment threshhold with different experiences and skills.

Some of the people we interviewed endorsed this assessment. A general foreman provided a graphic description:

> Take a boy baby and a girl baby. Expose the girl to cooking, cleaning, looking after the other kids, and so on. Expose the boy to fixing bicycles, mowing the grass, etcetera. Now at age 18, people are trained in opposite directions their whole life. You can't just take them and make them equal."

Such background differences may provde the canvas on which stereotypic judgments can be displayed. As Walshok has suggested, "There seem to be two common assumptions working against the entry of women: (1) special basic skills and aptitudes are required to succeed in the field, and (2) people who are acceptable to work in this field should have demonstrated prior interest and involvement in it" (Walshok, 1981, p. 276). Such beliefs would limit the likelihood that employers would look beyond their traditional recruitment sources in seeking new workers. As a result, it is unlikely that women would be recruited easily through the regular channels. Thus on the one hand, many women are not aware of the opportunities in industry; on the other hand, many employers may not be disposed to seek workers who do not appear in the standard pools.

Faced with affirmative action pressures from the government, it became apparent to many companies that the traditional sources of recruitment would not be sufficient to raise the percentage of women to the stipulated levels, particularly in the heavily male-dominated craft occupations. Two different strategies for dealing with this problem were chosen by the companies that we studied. Although different in philosophy and operation, both proved successful in bringing some women into craft jobs.

Company-Affiliated Training School

In one company, a separate training school was established by the company for the express purpose of providing a source of craft-trained minority and women workers. Originally, it was thought that all students in this school would be from outside the company, because the company itself had relatively few minorities or women to feed into the program. This plan was altered, however, after negotiations with the United Steelworkers Union, and in the revised plan only 50 percent of each class were nonemployees. These nonemployees were referred to the program under a Comprehensive Employment and Training Act (CETA) program and were paid minimum wage from funds of that program. The remaining 50 percent of the class were plant employees, chosen through a bidding system based on seniority. These members were paid their regular salary from company funds. Further provisions assured that the training program would achieve the goal of increasing minority and female representation. In each class, 50 percent of the students were minorities and/or women, thus adhering to the terms of the steel industry consent decree.

The training program itself lasted for approximately 1 year—specifically, four 12-week quarters with a 1-week break between each quarter. During these 1-week periods, students from the CETA program were taken to the steel mill to observe actual steelmaking operations. For the remainder of the program, the students were at a location away from the mill, in a facility consisting of a classroom area and a laboratory equipped with test and demonstration equipment similar to that in the mills. Approximately half of the time was spent in classroom sessions; the remaining time was devoted to laboratory work.

When students graduated from this program, they went to the mill and, if openings were available, moved into the craft positions for which they had trained. If craft openings did not exist, the employees returned to their former jobs and waited for appropriate openings in crafts. Theoretically, the CETA students were not guaranteed jobs if craft positions did not exist. In practice, however, nearly all were placed in craft jobs.

The success of this program was contingent on a rising employment pattern. In fact, the program has been abandoned in the past few years, due in part to a lack of in-plant demand for millwrights and motor inspectors. There were some criticisms of the program as well. Perhaps the major concern was whether the one-year training program, physically removed from the plant, gave employees sufficient skills in their chosen craft. Some supervisors, and some of the graduates of the training program as well, felt that not enough was learned—that although "book" learning was ample, there was not enough "hands-on" experience. "I'm not really a mechanic," one graduate of the program told us, and others echoed his statement.

At the same time, there were many positive aspects to the program. Students enjoyed the informal atmosphere of the training center and seemed to benefit from the personal attention that they received. Particularly for women and minorities, such an environment would appear to allow an easy transition into the steel industry. A small group in a congenial atmosphere, surrounded by peers who are learning, rather than by old guard who may be either suspicious or challenging—these would seem to be characteristics that would facilitate the entry of women into craft positions. And indeed, many of the women (and men as well) were laudatory in their description of their training experience.

The program was clearly effective in bringing women into the craft sequences. Prior to the training program, most newcomers to crafts at this company were recruited from trade schools. Not surprisingly, few of these recruits were women. In contrast, the training school, in its five years of operation, brought over 100 females into craft positions. Nearly two-thirds of these women entered through the now-defunct CETA sponsorship, and thus were new to the steel industry as well as to crafts. Many, we can assume, would not otherwise have found their way to the blue-collar jobs of the steel industry.

Formal Apprentice Programs

In the other company studied, craft people were trained either through a handyman-helper program or through the formal apprentice training program. Handyman-helper is an older concept, with less formally outlined procedures. A novice is placed in the role of an assistant, and informally acquires the skills of the trade. Progression from the handyman-maintenance helper to journeyman or craft status is indeterminate in length, depending solely on business conditions and job openings. Further, because the training is received in a specific department under specific supervisors, mobility is somewhat limited, as the acquired skills tend to be specific to that environment. Few women in the study were in this particular craft channel.

In contrast, the apprenticeship training program is formally defined, specifying the number of hours and steps through which an apprentice must move. For example, the standard millwright program consists of 7,280 hours of apprenticeship training, or approximately 3.5 years. In addition to this period of on-the-job training, apprentice programs are generally combined with a related education program, often conducted by a local university.

People bid to enter the apprentice programs, and acceptance is based in large part on seniority. Typically, there are far more bids than openings, and thus women with low seniority are often not accepted into the program as rapidly. Some women, and some men as well, are also reluctant to enter the formal training program because of the time demands and the reduced pay that is involved during the training period. For these and other reasons, including the relatively low number of women in the labor force, companies may have difficulty in getting women into the craft sequences, despite the provisions of the EEOC agreement.

To increase the pool of women, one of the companies in the study hired the services of an outside nonprofit recruiting agency. This agency attempted to identify and recruit apprentice prospects who were either female or members of minority groups. After screening potential candidates and selecting the most promising, they then conducted a six- to eight-week training program, aimed at upgrading the skills of candidates to the level necessary to pass the apprentice entry exams. Classes in this program met approximately eight hours per week and consisted of tutoring in mathematics, mechanical principles, and spatial relationships.

Some of the students in this program (about 40 percent) were already working in the steel industry and were often referred to the program by the company after they had failed the apprenticeship entry exam. Alternatively, students could apply to the program on their own because they wished to prepare for the entrance exams. The majority of the members of the training program, however, were not currently working in the steel industry and typically had no previous experience in that setting.

Although these nonemployees were second to the current employees in terms of the limited number of slots in the training program, there was room for many of them. Yet many others were turned away, in part due to the stringent screening requirements that the agency imposed. For example, in 1977–78, over 1250 people applied to the agency; only 340 of these were subsequently enrolled in the tutorial sessions. (Of these, about 75 percent actually completed the program.)

Once people completed the tutorial program, they were referred to the company for apprentice testing. Testifying to the quality of the preparation, slightly more than 80 percent of the agency's referrals passed the test for their chosen craft training program. Actual entrance into a training program, however, again depends on the availability of openings. In the period of our study, only 10 percent of these nonemployee graduates of the agency program were hired directly into craft openigns. Approximately two-thirds were hired into the company where they could bid for craft openings when such openings became available. The remaining 25 percent of the training school graduates had not been hired when we completed our study. Given the negative economic situation that has continued to develop since our study, it is unlikely that they have been hired in the intervening period.

Although entrance into the craft occupations is still limited, even with training from the outside agency, this agency has served as the principal source of women for this particular company. More than half of all female apprentices in the company were recruited through and trained by this agency.

The Value of Nontraditional Programs

Although our sample is small, based on only two companies within a major industry and on two very different approaches to nontraditional craft training, it appears to us that such nontraditional programs have considerable value in bringing women into craft occupations. Both of these programs, although different in their methods, were able to identify women not currently employed in the steel industry who could be trained for craft positions. In one instance, a pretraining tutorial program familiarized women with skills and concepts they had not previously acquired; in the other case, a low-pressure, congenial training program aided in the transition.

Corroborating these findings, other investigators have recently pointed to the importance of nontraditional channels for bringing women into the crafts. Briggs (1981), in surveying women in apprentice programs in the state of Wisconsin, suggests a number of factors that are likely to predict success for women in the skilled trades. Among these are participating in a preapprenticeship program; being guided by an informal knowledgeable support system; and having an opportunity to learn to use tools and practice the skills of the trade prior to the formal apprenticeship (Briggs, 1981, p. 130). Kane and Miller, surveying a broader range of outreach programs, conclude that "a system must be devised to recruit and prepare many more women capable of becoming apprentices" (1981, p. 102; see also Cook, 1980). As O'Farrell concludes in summarizing the results of several studies:

> More women are successfully recruited and placed and more women complete apprenticeship where there are special outreach, skill development, training, and counseling programs. These programs are particularly

important in this time of transition, as the first women are entering the trades and breaking down initial barriers. (1981, p. 151)

This time qualification is an important one. Twenty years from now, optimistically speaking, such programs may not be needed. Yet until vocational training programs, high school counselors, and society's expectations change, many women will probably not readily consider the industrial crafts as a reasonable occupational choice. Until they do, efforts to insure equality of opportunity must also include some devotion to recruitment and to precraft familiarization and orientation. Such strategies are not beneficial only to women. Minority group members may also have less access or less familiarity with the craft occupations and similar pre-entrance efforts may be equally successful there. Further, as Walshok (1981) has argued, entrance into crafts must be followed by specific compentency-based training and evaluation procedures that will allow for on-the-job training, ensuring that all workers indeed acquire the skills of the craft in an evenhanded manner.

10

Implications and Outlooks

Women employed outside the home in the United States have increased their numbers dramatically in recent decades, and all projections indicate that the percentage of women employed will continue to grow in the next decade as well. Yet despite this rise in employment, women have not been successful in achieving income equality with men. On the average, women continue to earn approximately 60 percent of what men do. Indeed, since the enactment of the Equal Pay Act of 1963, the disparity between male and female wages has actually become greater (Ratner, 1980).

A major reason for this disparity is the difference in pay for jobs in traditionally male-dominated fields and the pay received by those working in traditionally female-dominated fields. There are at least two approaches to altering this discrepancy. One concerns the issue of equal pay for work of equal value, or the question of comparable worth (cf. Remick, 1980; Helberger, 1980). Using this approach, one essentially attempts to compare apples and oranges, by defining a common metric through job analysis. The problems inherent in this controversial strategy are considerable. Beyond the difficulties in determining which dimensions of job performance are to be valued, there are a host of attendant problems that include the cost factors of implementing such a system and its acceptance by workers.

A more direct approach to occupational segregation, and theoretically a simpler one, is to increase the number of women in the higher-paying, male-dominated occupations. Such has been the aim of equal employment opportunity and affirmative action programs. The 1974 consent decree signed by the federal government, several large steel firms, and the United Steelworkers of America, is one example of this strategy. By increasing female employment in basic steel, the highest-wage manufacturing industry in the United States, one could begin to reduce the gap between male and female incomes. Such a strategy, if successful in this industry, could then act as a prototype for similar implementation in other high-paying and male-dominated sectors of the economy.

In describing "Women of Steel," we have attempted to analyze the effects of this policy. Although our findings are in some respects preliminary, we believe there are a number of important implications. In this chapter, we will discuss some of these implications, looking at the issues for policymakers, the outlook for women in blue-collar jobs, and questions for investigators who want to study these issues further.

PERSPECTIVES ON POLICY

Our analysis of the policy implications will consider two questions: first, the evidence obtained in this study, and second, the outlook for future policy issues.

Evidence

It is clear that the 1974 steel industry consent decree had positive effects on those groups targeted by the initiative. Prior to 1974, female employment in the industry was low and relatively constant. Subsequent to the consent decrees (but prior to the recession of the past few years), female employment climbed steadily. Some portion of this increase would probably have taken place even without the consent decrees, as a result of the general rise in female employment, the attention given by the women's movement to occupational issues, and other societal shifts. In fact, female employment at one of our two study companies did show an increase prior to the consent decrees, a consequence, according to company officials, of an insufficient number of men in the available labor pool.

Yet it it quite unlikely that the increase in female employment would have been as sharp without the intervention of the federal government. As Ratner (1980) notes, "Regardless of how a law or other government regulation defines discrimination or specifies procedures for remedying it, the most important stimulus to change within firms appears to be the threat of costly government sanctions for noncompliance" (1980, p. 426). Consent decrees represent a form of "settling out of court," avoiding the more costly litigation that a court hearing would entail. Further evidence of the effectiveness of the consent decree in the steel industry are the comparisons with female employment in blue-collar jobs in other comparable industries, where change has been much less noticeable (see Chapter 6).

The success of the firms studied in meeting affirmative action goals for hiring women was contingent on at least two factors. First, during the period of study, employment was rising at both of the study companies. Strong employment prospects are a precondition for getting a significant number of women into the steel industry. If firms are reducing employment, as virtually all steel firms have done in 1981 and 1982, it is impossible to increase employment of women. The strongly held policy of laying off and recalling on the basis of seniority in the steel industry makes it especially difficult to alter the sex structure of employment except under conditions of expanding employment. Indeed, female employment in the industry is now lower than it was prior to the adoption of the consent decree stipulations.

Rising employment also allows a company to increase the rate of hiring women without deleterious effects on other previously targeted groups of employees. Using both national figures as well as the data from our two study companies, we found that in terms of absolute numbers, both black and Hispanic males continued to gain jobs during the period following the consent decree, despite the emphasis on hiring females. However, it should also be noted that the relative share of jobs held by minority males did decrease at the one company that had a substantial proportion of black and Hispanic male workers. (White males also showed a decreased share over this period, although in only one of the companies did their absolute numbers decrease.) It is of course inevitable that relative shares of incumbent groups will decrease if a new group is added to those dividing the "pie." However, the negative effects of this alteration are probably minimized as long as absolute numbers continue to increase. Without rising employment, of course, such continued increases are not possible.

A second factor related to the implementation of affirmative action programs for women in blue-collar employment appears to be the existence of specific outreach programs. Particularly in more specialized areas such as the craft occupations, simply establishing an affirmative action goal may not be sufficient to attract women to these fields. The barriers of tradition, previous experience, and lack of knowledge as to what these jobs entail may not be surmounted without additional effort.

In both of the companies that we studied, specific outreach programs were established to recruit female workers into the craft occupations. Although these two programs were quite different in form, both attempted to identify new sources for recruiting employees and provided special training for women to compensate for previous deficits.

It is particularly difficult to significantly affect the sex (or race) composition of those occupations, like the crafts, that require long periods of training. In our study, the majority of craft women were in some stage of an apprentice or handyman-helper training period when they were interviewed. Given recent layoffs, it is unlikely that many of these women still remain in the work force. In a cyclical industry with declining blue-collar employment, it is extremely difficult to provide large numbers of apprentice openings. Indeed, most apprenticeship training in the steel industry is currently "on hold." Thus those positions that require the most skill and are among the best paid—and that were, in fact, most directly targeted by the consent decrees—at the same time represent the goals most difficult to achieve.

Outlook

An analysis of the effects of affirmative action for women in the steel industry is a picture of contrasts. On the one hand, the available evidence suggests that the policy was an effective one, contributing to sharp rises in female employment in the industry. An energetic and committed implementation of equal opportunity and affirmative action programs can have positive employment effects for the target groups without serious harm to the employers. The preponderance of the evidence in our study suggests that the lack of women in the steel industry has historical origins, rather than being due to an inability of women to perform adequately in contemporary steel mills. Public policy may play a very constructive role in nudging organizations to overcome historically based practices that exclude or limit participation of particular groups in specific industries or occupations.

At the same time, the current economic climate has effectively eliminated all gains made by women during the targeting period. Although declining steel industry employment is related to the current depressed state of the United States and world economies, it is widely forecast that industry employment will never regain former levels. Given the existent policies of layoff and recall based on seniority, the situation does not augur well for steelworkers hired in recent years. Nearly all of the female blue-collar workers in the industry are in this category.

Thus economic conditions are a precondition of overriding importance for effective affirmative action. We would suggest that industries and occupations in which employment is expanding are much better targets for specific affirmative action initiatives than are stable or declining industries. Similarly, highly cyclical industries will find it more difficult to provide permanent new employment opportunities than will more stable industries. These market considerations should be taken into account by policymakers when planning affirmative action programs.

Particular consideration should be given to these factors when the focus of policy is on occupations that require long periods of training, such as the craft jobs in the steel industry. Managers and policymakers might consider a number of strategies to overcome this problem. One possibility is the support and encouragement of new forms of craft training, specifically ones designed to shorten the required period of training. A shorter (but not necessarily less comprehensive) program could allow people to develop needed skills more rapidly, thus overcoming some of the problems caused by the cyclical nature of the industry. The adoption of policies that encourage more broadly based training could also open more craft opportunities for women and minorities who are caught in an economic downturn. If craft workers have greater mobility among industries, they will be better able to move into steady craft employment than if they must rely on a single, perhaps declining, industry. Although steel companies have traditionally favored training craft workers in intracompany programs, the recent agreement to establish industry-wide apprentice programs is a step in the suggested direction. Extending this development beyond the boundaries of a single industry would be a further step in the same direction.

Our analysis of affirmative action policies for women in the steel industry also alert us to possible policy conflicts in the future. In considering the effects of current policies, we looked for potential negative effects on other previously targeted minority groups. In the expanding employment situation that we studied, such effects were minimal. Yet future policymakers should not ignore the possible conflicts inherent in ignoring one mandate while following another. The current interest in age discrimination is a case in point. If public policymakers were to instigate a broad program focusing on age discrimination, it is probable that both women and minority men would find reduced employment opportunities. Initiatives aimed at correcting age discrimination are by definition aimed at protecting the worker over 40 years of age. In most organizations, those workers are largely white males. Thus a focus on age discrimination will primarily protect older white males and will have negative overall effects for women and minority males, many of whom are in the "under-40" group. The severity of these conflicts again depends on general economic conditions and on the health of the specifically targeted industry. Both the general issue and the more specific conditions need to be considered by policymakers concerned with forming and implementing equal opportunity legislation, to insure that such legislation does indeed provide equal opportunity for all.

PERSPECTIVES ON FEMALE EMPLOYMENT

In assessing the implications for female employment, we can again look first at the direct and indirect evidence from our study and then at the outlook for future employment.

Evidence

Given the opportunity, it appears that women were able to perform most blue-collar jobs in the steel plants reasonably well. Although no objective performance data were available, the views of male and female workers, and of management, supported the assertion that most women could perform most steel jobs at an acceptable level. Thus just as the earlier predictions of some industry executives that the slighter stature of the Japanese would not enable them to become major producers of steel proved wrong, so the fear that women could not do the job appears to have been exaggerated.

Furthermore, most women appear to like their jobs in the mills. It is interesting to note that, with few exceptions, the responses that we received from women were very similar to those that we received from men in areas such as self-evaluation, job likes and dislikes, and job aspirations. Turnover figures were more favorable for women than men, again providing evidence for the ability and willingness of women to work in this setting. Among all plant personnel that we interviewed, there was general agreement that one's attitudes toward the job and coworkers are the most important determinant of success. Although "attitudes" are undoubtedly multidetermined and difficult to assess, it is important that one's attitudes are controllable. Were a less controllable characteristic such as physical strength the main determinant, women would be at an inevitable disadvantage. In contrast, explanations focusing on the worker's own personality or motivation, while not making success automatic, nonetheless allow women workers a fair opportunity.

The issue of physical strength is an important one because it has been so central to debates on the suitability of women for jobs in heavy industry. Women are, on the average, not as strong as men. Although the "average" woman may not apply for steel mill employment, there is also evidence that male and female steelworkers differ in physical capabilities (Arnold et al., 1982). The importance of this differential must be interpreted in the context of the job demands.

The two mills that we studied are among the most modern in the United States. As a result, the number of jobs requiring great physical strength is more limited and the number of jobs involving use of automated equipment is greater, as compared to less modern steel plants. Under these conditions, any differential in physical strength did not appear to affect the performance of women in many jobs. Yet even in highly automated steel plants, there are still some jobs requiring considerable physical strength. It is widely believed that women do not perform these jobs as well as men, and Arnold's data (Arnold et al., 1982) would support this belief.

In assessing the evidence that women did find increasing opportunities for employment within the steel industry, one should also consider where progress did not occur. Our findings point to at least two areas of concern. First, there is little evidence that women are moving into supervisory ranks in the plants that we studied. Only two of more than one hundred supervisors that we interviewed were women. In one instance, management had suggested that almost no women were interested in such positions. However our interviews suggested that some female workers—and not substantially fewer than men—would in fact like some form of supervisory job.

It seems quite likely that negative judgments about the capability of women, previously held with regard to any form of work in the mills, may persist when consideration is given to openings in supervision. Such beliefs may also affect day-to-day decisions, as when a worker is called up to assume the role of "subforeman" on a temporary basis. Such experiences, generally a forerunner of more permanent appointments, are still being denied most women. Recent layoffs again threaten the progress of women in this regard and suggest that significant numbers of women in supervision will not be evident for years to come.

A second area of concern in the female employment picture is the number of women we interviewed who were doing janitorial work. Despite the fact that their formal position was one of laborer, the work that they did was very different from, and considerably easier than, that done by other male and female workers. Furthermore, the position of janitor lies in its own cul-de-sac, removed from the floor and the normal interchange of workers. Hence women in these positions are unlikely to gain skills needed for other, more skilled, more prestigious, or better-paying jobs within the mills.

It is not possible to state with certainty whether this concentration of women in janitorial jobs was due to preferences of the women themselves or to discriminatory assignments on the part of supervisors. On the one hand, managers often suggested that some women preferred janitorial work and that the work was more suitable for them. On the other hand, the women we interviewed often believed that some supervisors routinely assign women to traditional female jobs because of their own stereotypes and prejudices. Consideration of the demographic characteristics of the female janitors, while pointing to a distinguishable pattern, does not resolve this question either. On the average, women performing janitorial jobs were less likely to be white, more likely to be Hispanic, older, and to have dependents. Such characteristics may serve to define a subgroup of women who prefer the less taxing demands and more regular hours of the janitorial assignment. Alternatively, this constellation of characteristics may fit a supervisory stereotype as to who should do janitorial work. Both positions may account for a portion of the total pattern.

Outlook

Although their future employment picture within the steel industry is bleak, women have found that they can work in the male-dominated heavy industries of this country. To be sure, their entrance has not been without difficulty. Reports of negative attitudes and behaviors by coworkers and incidents of sexual harassment accompany the feelings of accomplishment that many women have. Yet if women can succeed in this industry, with its image of "John Henry" and its tradition of male dominance, then their prospects for other industries seem strong.

Given the increasing level of technology that is characterizing most industries, it seems clear that women have the capacity to increase their representation in other previously male-dominated industries. The rapid increase in robotics that is forecast for U.S. industry should mean that even fewer jobs require the physical strength that they once did. Given the capability of women to perform most jobs in these industries, only tradition can hamper their successful performance.

Tradition is not always so easily overcome, however. The woman who enters a traditionally male field must still cope with pockets of resistance. It is not clear how extensive such resistance is. In one company that we studied, immediate supervisors were significantly more positive about women's capabilities than were the more remote superintendents. Such findings would suggest that direct experience with blue-collar women is successful in modifying previously negative beliefs. To counterbalance this finding, in the other company, where the proportion of women was greater and their tenure longer, supervisors were more negative about the effect of women on productivity than were supervisors in the "less-integrated" company. Thus there are still mixed signals, not surprising, perhaps, in view of the relative novelty of women's entrance.

Given this mixture of signals, women can not expect red carpets to be laid down. Entrance into male-dominated occupations will still take a great deal of effort, both individually and collectively. Federal mandates may be necessary if good intentions do not come to the fore. "Women of steel" have proven that it can be done, however. "Women of robotics" may transform the novelty to commonplace.

PROSPECTIVES FOR RESEARCH

Blue-collar workers, both male and female, have been ignored compared to their white-collar counterparts. Decisions regarding job and occupation made in these sectors are probably not best modeled by career development sequences formulated for mangerial personnel. Yet such decisions should be of interest, particularly in an economy that is shifting from dominance by heavy industries to a high-technology emphasis. How will workers make the transition from one sphere to another?

More specifically, the decisions of women to enter traditionally male fields of industry have for the most part been given no notice. Our own research merely scratched the surface of this issue. As others, such as Walshok (1981) have found, women entering blue-collar and craft fields do not show a predictable line of progression. The backgrounds of women in these fields are extremely diverse, and their previous work experience often shows no "logical" link to their current jobs. Models of job selection must be altered to account for these kinds of patterns, particularly as women move into new terrain.

From a research point of view, it is also worth noting how few sex differences were found in this research. With few exceptions, men and women responded quite similarly to our questions. Laboratory research often reports differences between males and females on a variety of behavioral and self-evaluative dimensions (although even there, differences are not as common nor as sizable as many people imagine, cf. Deaux, 1982). Although randomly selected samples of males and females may show certain differences, it is not safe to assume that self-selected groups of men and women will show the same differences. Women and men who choose to work in the steel industry may share far more similarities than they show differences. Early research results suggest that the same statement could be made for male and female managers, male and female professors, and the like. Differences that are observed may be due less to characteristics inherent in the male and female, and may be due more to influences emanating from those who believe they are different.

Working women are here to stay. In years past, the questions of whether women would work and why they would work were at the forefront of investigator's concerns. For the years ahead, what they will do and how they will do it seem much more critical questions.

In this study, we have attempted to describe how and what one selected group of women—the women of steel—are doing today. Although the years covered in this study may prove to be the pinnacle of employment for women steelworkers for some years to come, the knowledge gained from this exploration should provide some base for understanding future generations of women workers.

Appendixes

Appendix A

Interview Form
for Workers

The first set of questions is about your job in general.

1. What is the title of the job you usually work?
2. Please tell me briefly what you do on the job you usually work.
3. How many people do the same job that you do in this department?
4. What is your present work schedule? Straight shift? Rotating shift?
5. Do you usually work with a group of people, or usually alone? (always with a group, usually with a group, usually alone, always alone)
   5a. If with a group, about how many people are in the group you work with?
   5b. If with a group, are these usually the same people or usually different people in your work group from day to day?
6. What do you like best about the job you usually work?
7. What do you like least about the job you usually work?
8. Think about when you first started working at this plant. What was the hardest thing to get used to about working here?
9. If you could have any job in this department, what job would you most like to have?
   9a. Why would you like to have that particular job?

10. Are there any jobs in this department that you would not want to have?

10a. (if yes) What jobs?

10b. (if yes) Why would you not want those jobs?

11. If you could work in any department, what department would you most like to work in?

11a. Why would you like to work in that particular department?

12. Are there departments that you would not like to work in?

12a. (if yes) What departments?

12b. (if yes) Why wouldn't you want to work in those departments?

13. Is your job harder or easier than other jobs in your department? (Scale provided: 5=much easier, 4=somewhat easier, 3=about the same, 2=somewhat harder, 1=much harder)

14. Consider the job you usually work. What types of physical activity are involved?

15. What is the heaviest thing you have to lift by hand in the job you usually work?

15a. How much does it weigh?

15b. How often do you have to lift it?

16. Consider the job you usually work. How much physical strength does your job require? (Scale provided: 4=extreme amount, 3=quite a bit, 2=a slight amount, 1=very little)

17. Overall, how much do you like your job? (Scale provided: 4=extremely well, 3=quite well, 2=slightly well, 1=not at all)

18. What are the most important things that help a person do your job well?

19. How important is each of the following things in determining how well a person does your job? (Scale provided for each of the following questions: 4=extremely important, 3=quite important, 2=slightly important, 1=not at all important)

    a. The person's previous work experience

    b. The person's vocational or technical training

    c. The person's formal education

    d. The person's physical endurance

    e. The person's physical strength

    f. The person's attitudes toward coworkers

    g. The person's length of time in the department

    h. The person's ability to deal with hazing

    i. The person's attitude toward the immediate supervisor

    j. The attitudes of coworkers toward the person

    k. The attitude of the immediate supervisor toward the person

    l. The attitude of department supervision toward the person

Now I would like to ask you some questions about how you do your job.

20. How good are you at your job compared to other people who do the same kind of work? (Much better, somewhat better, about the same, somewhat worse, much worse)

21. Are there any things that could be done to help you do your job better? If yes, please explain.

22. Here is a list of ways in which workers may differ. For each thing, please compare yourself to other workers who do the same kind of work. (Scale provided for each of the following questions: 5=much better, 4=somewhat better, 3=about the same, 2=somewhat worse, 1=much worse)
    a. Your work experience
    b. Your vocational or technical training
    c. Your formal education
    d. Your physical endurance
    e. Your physical strength
    f. Your attitude toward your coworkers
    g. Your ability to deal with hazing
    h. Your attitude toward your immediate supervisor

23.. Consider the attitudes of other people toward you. Tell me how good or bad these attitudes are. (Scale provided for each of the following questions: 5=very good, 4=somewhat good, 3=neither good nor bad, 2=somewhat bad, 1=very bad)
    a. The attitude of your immediate supervisor toward you
    b. The attitude of the department supervisor toward you
    c. The attitudes of your coworkers toward you

The next few questions are about the craft occupations.

24. Is your job a craft or a production job?
(*Questions 25 and 26 answered only by production workers*)

25. Have you ever applied to an apprenticeship or craft training program here?

25a. (if yes) What happened?

25b. (if no) Are there any particular reasons you have chosen not to apply to an apprenticeship or craft training program?

26. Do you think you would ever apply to an apprenticeship or craft training program here in the future?

26a. (if yes) Why would you want to go into an apprenticeship or craft training program here?

(*Questions 27 through 40 answered only by craft workers*)

27. Are you an apprentice, a helper, or a full craftsman?

27a. (if apprentice or helper) When did you begin your apprenticeship or craft training program?

27b. (if craftsman) What kind of program did you take to become a craft person?

27c. (if craftsman) When did you complete your apprenticeship or craft training program?

28. Why did you choose to enter a craft occupation?

29. Why did you choose this craft rather than some other craft occupation?

30. How did you learn about your apprenticeship or training program?

31. Did you go through special training to take the entrance tests for your apprenticeship or other craft training program?

31a. (if yes) What sort of training?

31b. (if yes) Who was most helpful to you in preparing to pass any tests you had to take to enter apprentice training?

31c. How hard or easy were the craft entry tests? (Scale provided: 5=very easy, 4=somewhat easy, 3=neither easy nor hard, 2=somewhat hard, 1=very hard)

32. What did (do) you like best about your apprenticeship or craft training program?

33. What did (do) you like least about your apprenticeship or craft training program?

34. What, if anything, could have been changed to make your apprenticeship or craft training program better for you?

35. In your apprenticeship or craft training program, how hard or easy was the on-the-job training? (Scale provided: 5=very easy, 4=somewhat easy, 3=neither easy nor hard, 2=somewhat hard, 1=very hard)

36. In your apprenticeship program, how hard or easy were the tests given in related education. (Scale provided: 5=very easy, 4=somewhat easy, 3=neither easy nor hard, 2=somewhat hard, 1=very hard)

37. During your apprenticeship period, how many journeymen have supervised your training?

38. Describe the relationship between you and the journeyman who supervised you the most.

38a. (if more than one journeyman) Tell me about your relationship with the other journeymen who worked with you.

39. How good or bad was the relationship between you and the

journeyman who supervised you the most? (Scale provided: 5=very good, 4=somewhat good, 3=neither good nor bad, 2=somewhat bad, 1=very bad)

40. In general, would you recommend your craft training program to other workers?

40a. (if no) Why not?

The next few questions are about your opinions and experiences with women in the steel mills.

41. How many women do you have contact with during a normal work shift?

41a. (if more than zero) What do these women do?

42. Is your immediate supervisor a woman or a man?

43. Are there any jobs in your department that some supervisors generally do not assign to women?

43a. (if yes) Which jobs?

43b. (if yes) Why don't these supervisors generally assign these particular jobs to women?

44. Are there jobs in your department that some supervisors generally do not assign to men?

44a. (if yes) Which jobs?

44b. (if yes) Why don't these supervisors generally assign those particular jobs to men?

45. Your department currently employs more women than it employed in the past. What effect, if any, has the increase in women had in the following areas? (Scale provided for each of the following questions: greatly reduced, moderately reduced, slightly reduced, no effect, slightly increased, moderately increased, greatly increased)

   a. Your ability to do your job
   b. Quality of work done in your department
   c. Worker morale
   d. Cooperation among workers
   e. Overall productivity

45a. Could you briefly explain your reasons for these ratings? For example, are your ratings based on your own observations and experiences, on the comments of other people, or on some available reports?

46. Are there any problems that women in particular have or would have working in your department?

46a. (if yes) What problems?

46b. (if yes) Considering the problems that women have in your department, what if anything should be done to solve these problems?

47. Now consider work in the steel mills in general. It may be similar or different from work in your own department. Are there any problems that women in particular have or would have working in the steel mills in general?

47a. (if yes) What problems?

48. In your opinion, what are the most important things that determine whether a woman will succeed in the steel mills?

49. Do you think this company makes special efforts to hire the following people?

    Black women?

    Hispanic women?

    White women?

    Black men?

    Hispanic men?

    White men?

In the next few questions, I will ask you for some information about yourself. Remember that all information will be kept absolutely confidential.

50. When did you begin working in this department?

51. When were you first employed by this company?

52. Have you ever worked at any other steel mill before this one?

52a. (if yes) When?

52b. (if yes) For how long?

53. Where did you work before you worked at this steel mill?

53a. What was your job there?

54. Does or did your mother work outside her home?

54a. (if yes) What is or was her job?

55. Does or did your father work outside his home?

55a. (if yes) What is or was his job?

56. Do you have any (other) relatives who work in a steel mill?

56a. (if yes) How are they related to you?

57. Are you the sole wage earner in your household?

58. Do you have any children or other dependents?

58a. (if yes) How many?

58b. (if yes) What are their ages?

58c. (if yes) How do your work and family schedules fit together?

59. What is your date of birth?

60. What was the last grade in school that you finished?

61. Do you have any comments or suggestions about the interview or anything we talked about?

Appendix B

Interview Form
for Supervisors

1. Currently, what are your area's (department's) most important operating problems?

2. What are your area's (department's) goals for the current year?

3. What are the most important things that determine how well a person does on the job in your area (department)?

4. How important is each of the following things in determining how well a person does in your area (department)? (Scale provided for each of the following questions: 4=extremely important, 3=quite important, 2=slightly important, 1=not at all important)

   a. The person's previous work experience
   b. The person's vocational training
   c. The person's formal education
   d. The person's physical endurance
   e. The person's physical strength
   f. The person's attitude toward coworkers
   g. The person's length of time in the department
   h. The person's ability to deal with hazing
   i. The person's attitudes toward the immediate supervisor
   j. The attitudes of coworkers toward the person
   k. The attitude of the immediate supervisor toward the person

l. The attitude of department supervision toward the person

5. Here are some suggestions for improving the performance of workers in steel mill jobs. How much would each of these things improve the performance of workers in your area (department)? (Scale provided for each of the following questions: 4=extreme improvement, 3=quite a bit of improvement, 2=slight improvement, 1=no improvement)

    a. Hire people who have more experience in similar work settings
    b. Hire people who have more vocational training
    c. Hire people who have more formal education
    d. Hire people who have more physical endurance
    e. Hire people who have more physical strength
    f. Give workers training in how to deal with hazing by coworkers
    g. Give workers physical conditioning training for improving their strength and endurance
    h. Give supervisors training in working with mixed groups of workers; such as blacks and whites, men and women
    i. Give workers training in how to work together in mixed groups of men and women, blacks and whites, etc.

6. How important is on-the-job experience in the department in improving worker performance? (Scale provided: 4=extremely important, 3=quite important, 2=slightly important, 1=not at all important)

7. Are there any other ways in which the performance of workers in your area (department) could be improved?

    7a. (if yes) What are these other ways?

8. Consider all the jobs in your area (department): supervisory, general labor, operating personnel, maintenance, and clerical. Are there any jobs that women generally do better than men?

    8a. (if yes) Which jobs?

    8b. (if yes) In what ways are women better than men at these jobs?

9. Are there any jobs in your area (department) that men and women do equally well?

    9a. (if yes) Which jobs?

10. Are there any jobs in your area (department) that men generally do better than women?'

    10a. (if yes) Which jobs?

    10b. (if yes) In what ways are men better than women at these jobs?

11. Are there any particular jobs in your area (department) that women generally avoid?

    11a. (if yes) What jobs?

    11b. (if yes) Why do you think that women avoid these jobs?

12. Are there any particular jobs in your area (department) that men generally avoid?

    12a. (if yes) What jobs?

12b. (if yes) Why do you think that men avoid these jobs?

13. Are there any particular jobs in your area (department) that women generally prefer?

13a. (if yes) What jobs?

13b. (if yes) Why do you think that women prefer these jobs?

14. Are there any particular jobs in your area (department) that men generally prefer?

14a. (if yes) What jobs?

14b. (if yes) Why do you think that men prefer these jobs?

15. Are there jobs in your department that some supervisors generally do not assign to women?

15a. (if yes) What jobs?

15b. (if yes) Why don't these supervisors generally assign women to these particular jobs?

16. Are there jobs in your department that some supervisors generally do not assign to men?

16a. (if yes) What jobs?

16b. (if yes) Why don't supervisors generally assign men to these particular jobs?

17. Your department currently employs more women than it employed in the past. What effect, if any, has the increase in women had in the following areas? (Scale provided for the following questions: greatly reduced, moderately reduced, slightly reduced, no effect, slightly increased, moderately increased, greatly increased)

    a. Training costs
    b. Supervision time
    c. Job assignment costs
    d. Absenteeism costs
    e. Turnover costs
    f. Maintenance costs
    g. Worker morale
    h. Cooperation among workers
    i. Overall productivity

18. If 20 percent (one of each five) of the employees in each occupation in your department were women, what effect, if any, would this have in the following areas? (Scale provided for each of the following questions: greatly reduced, moderately reduced, slightly reduced, no effect, slightly increased, moderately increased, greatly increased)

    a. Training costs
    b. Supervision time
    c. Job assignment costs
    d. Absenteeism costs
    e. Turnover costs

    f. Maintenance costs

    g. Worker morale

    h. Cooperation among workers

    i. Overall productivity

19. In your opinion, what are the most important things that determine whether a woman will succeed in the steel mills?

20. Are there any problems that women in particular have working in your area (department)?

    20a. (if yes) Please explain.

    20b. (if yes) Considering the problems that women have in your area (department), what, if anything, should be done to solve these problems?

Earlier I asked you how much certain things would improve the performance of workers in general in your area (department). Now I would like to ask you to consider the same suggestions for women workers only. It is possible that some of these things might be more or less important for women than for workers in general.

21. How much would each of these things improve the performance of women in your area (department)? (Scale provided for the following questions: 4=extreme improvement, 3=quite a bit of improvement, 2=slight improvement, 1=no improvement)

    a. Hire women who have more experience in similar work settings

    b. Hire women who have more vocational training

    c. Hire women who have more formal education

    d. Hire women who have more physical endurance

    e. Hire women who have more physical strength

    f. Give women training in how to deal with hazing by coworkers

    g. Give women training in how to deal with sexual harassment

    h. Give women physical conditioning training for improving their strength and endurance

    i. Give men workers training to be more accepting of women coworkers

    j. Give supervisors more training in working with women workers

    k. Better development or enforcement of policies aimed at preventing sexual harassment

22. How important is on-the-job experience in the department in improving women's performance? (Scale provided: 4=extremely, 3=quite, 2=slightly, 1=not at all)

23. Are there any other ways in which the performance of women in your area (department) could be improved?

23a. (if yes) What are these other ways?

Now I would like to ask you a few questions about your own background and experience. Remember that all information will be kept absolutely confidential.

24. When did you assume your present position?

25. When did you begin working in this department?

26. When were you first employed by this company?

27. What is your date of birth?

28. What is the highest grade of school or college that you completed?

29. Do you have any additional comments or opinions about any of the issues that we've talked about?

Bibliography

Abbott, E. *Women in industry. A study in American economics history.* New York: D. Appleton, 1910.

Allen, W. R. Family roles, occupational statuses, and achievement orientations among Black women in the United States. *Signs,* 1979, *4,* 670–686.

Almond, P. U.S. steelmakers try to catch up on new technology. *The Cleveland Press,* August 18, 1981, p. A4.

Almquist, E. M., Women in the labor force. *Signs,* 1977, *2,* 843–855.

Almquist, E. M., & Wehrle-Einhorn, J. L. The doubly disadvantaged: Minority women in the labor force. In A. H. Stromberg & S. Harkess (Eds.), *Women working: Theories and facts in perspective.* Palo Alto, Calif.: Mayfield, 1978. Pp. 63–88.

American Iron and Steel Institute, *Annual statistical report.* Washington, D.C.: American Iron and Steel Institute, 1982.

American Iron and Steel Institute, *Steel at the crossroads: The American steel industry in the 1980s.* Washington, D.C.: American Iron and Steel Institute, January 1980.

Arnold, J. D., Rauschenberger, J. M., Soubel, W. G., & Guion, R. M. Validation and utility of a strength test for selecting steelworkers. *Journal of Applied Psychology,* 1982, *67,* 588–604.

Augustine, J. Personnel turnover. In J. Famularo (Ed.), *Handbook of modern personnel administration.* New York: McGraw-Hill, 1972.

Bahr, S. J. Effects on family power and division of labor in the family. In L. W. Hoffman & F. I. Nye (Eds.), *Working mothers.* San Francisco: Jossey-Bass, 1974. Pp. 167–185.

Baker, S. H. Women in blue-collar and service occupations. In A. H. Stromberg & S. Harkess (Eds.), *Women working: Theories and facts in perspective.* Palo Alto, Calif.: Mayfield, 1978. Pp. 339–376.

Barrett, N. S. Women in the job market: Occupations, earnings, and career opportunities. In R. E. Smith (Ed.), *The subtle revolution: Women at work*. Washington, D.C.: The Urban Institute, 1979. Pp. 31–61.

Baxandall, R., Gordon, L., & Reverby, S. *America's working women*. New York: Vintage, 1976.

Bjorn, L., & Gruber, J. E. *Awareness of sex discrimination and sexual harassment among women auto workers: Some preliminary findings*. Unpublished manuscript. Dearborn, Mich.: University of Michigan, 1981.

Blau, F. D. The data on women workers, past, present, and future. In A. H. Stromberg & S. Harkess (Eds.), *Women working: Theories and facts in perspective*. Palo Alto, Calif.: Mayfield, 1978. Pp. 29–62.

Briggs, N. Overcoming barriers to successful entry and retention of women in traditionally male skilled blue-collar trades in Wisconsin. In V. M. Briggs, Jr., & F. F. Foltman (Eds.), *Apprenticeship research: Emerging findings and future trends*. Ithaca, N.Y.: New York State School of Industrial and Labor Relations, Cornell University, 1981. Pp. 106–131.

Bureau of Labor Statistics. *Handbook of labor statistics 1973*. Washington, D. C.: U. S. Department of Labor, 1973.

Bureau of Labor Statistics. *Working women: A chartbook*. Washington, D. C.: U. S. Department of Labor, 1975a.

Bureau of Labor Statistics. *Historical statistics of the United States*. Washington, D. C.: U.S. Department of Labor, 1975b.

Bureau of Labor Statistics. *Employment and unemployment during 1975*. Washington, D. C.: U. S. Department of Labor, 1976.

Bureau of Labor Statistics. *Employment and unemployment trends during 1977*. Washington, D. C.: U. S. Department of Labor, 1978.

Bureau of Labor Statistics. *Handbook of labor statistics, 1978*. Washington, D. C.: U. S. Department of Labor, 1979a.

Bureau of Labor Statistics. *Employment and unemployment during 1978: An analysis*. Washington, D. C.: U. S. Department of Labor, 1979b.

Bureau of Labor Statistics. *Women in the labor force: Some new data series*. Washington, D. C.: U. S. Department of Labor, 1979c.

Bureau of Labor Statistics. *Employment and unemployment during 1979: An analysis*. Washington, D. C.: U. S. Department of Labor, 1980.

Bureau of Labor Statistics. *Employment and unemployment: A report on 1980*. Washington, D. C.: U. S. Department of Labor, April 1981.

Bureau of Labor Statistics. *1981 weekly earnings of men and women compared in 100 occupations*. Washington, D. C.: U. S. Department of Labor, March 7, 1982.

Business Week, December 7, 1981.

Business Week, May 31, 1982.

Cook, A. H. Vocational training, the labor market, and the unions. In R. S. Ratner (Ed.), *Equal employment policy for women: Strategies for implementation in the United States, Canada, and Western Europe*. Philadelphia: Temple University Press, 1980. Pp. 199–226.

Crandall, R. W. *The U. S. Steel industry in recurrent crisis: Policy options in a competitive world*. Washington, D. C.: The Brookings Institution, 1981.

Crandall, V. C. Sex differences in expectancy of intellectual and academic reinforcement. In C. P. Smith (Ed.), *Achievement-related motives in children*. New York: Russell Sage, 1969.

Crosby, F. *Relative deprivation and working women*. New York: Oxford University Press, 1982.

Crowley, J. E. *Longitudinal and cross-cohort employment patterns of women*. Paper presented at meeting of American Psychological Association, Washington, D. C., August 1982.

Crowley, J., Levitan, T. E., & Quinn, R. P. Seven deadly half-truths about women. In C. Tavris (Ed.), *The female experience*. Del Mar, Calif.: CRM, 1973. Pp. 76-78.

Davis, R. H. *Life in the iron mills*. Old Westbury, N. Y.: The Feminist Press, 1972.

Deaux, K. *The behavior of women and men*. Monterey, Calif.: Brooks/Cole, 1976.

Deaux, K. Sex differences. In T. Blass (Ed.), *Personality variables in social behavior*. Hillsdale, N. J.: Erlbaum, 1977. Pp. 357–377.

Deaux, K. *From individual differences to social categories: Analysis of a decade's research on gender*. Presidential address presented at meeting of Midwestern Psychological Association, Minneapolis, May 1982.

Douglas, P. H. *Black working women: Factors affecting labor market experience*, working paper No. 39. Wellesley, Massachusetts: Center for Research on Women, 1980.

Dublin, T. *Women at work: The transformation of work and community in Lowell, Massachusetts, 1826–1860*. New York: Columbia University Press, 1979.

Dye, N. S. *As equals and as sisters*. Columbia, Miss.: University of Missouri Press, 1980.

Employment and Training Administration. *ETA Review*. Washington, D. C.: U. S. Department of Labor, July 1979.

Equal Employment Opportunity Commission. Letter and accompanying tables from James S. Noel, Survey Branch, to Joseph C. Ullman, November 10, 1980.

Faley, R. H. Sexual harassment: Critical review of legal cases with general principles and preventive measures. *Personnel Psychology*, 1982, in press.

Fleishman, E. A., & Hogan, J. C. *A taxonomic method for assessing the physical requirements of jobs: The physical abilities analysis approach*. Publication of Advanced Research Resources Organization, Washington, D. C., June 1978.

Fullerton, H. N., Jr. The 1995 labor force: A first look. *Monthly Labor Review*, 1980, *103* (12), 11–21.

Glueck, W. F. *Personnel: A diagnostic approach* (rev. ed.). Dallas: Business Publications, 1978.

Gordon, F., & Strober, M. (Eds.), *Bringing women into management*. New York: McGraw-Hill, 1975.

Greenberger, M. The effectiveness of Federal laws prohibiting sex discrimination in employment in the United States. In R. S. Ratner (Ed.), *Equal employment policy for women: Strategies for implementation in the United States, Canada, and Western Europe*. Philadelphia: Temple University Press, 1980. Pp. 108–128.

Grimm, J. W. Women in female-dominated professions. In A. H. Stromberg & S. Harkess (Eds.), *Women working: Theories and facts in perspective*. Palo Alto, Calif.: Mayfield, 1978. Pp. 293–315.

Gruber, J. E., & Bjorn, L. *Sexual harassment on the line: Harassment type, source, and response in the auto industry*. Paper presented at meeting of the American Sociological Association, Toronto, 1981.

Gurin, P. Labor market experiences and expectancies. *Sex Roles,* 1981, *7,* 1079–1092.

Gutek, B. A., Nakamura, C. Y., Gahart, M., Handschumacher, I., & Russell, D. Sexuality and the workplace. *Basic and Applied Social Psychology,* 1980, *1,* 255–265.

Gutek, B. A., & Nakamura, C. Y. Gender roles and sexuality in the world of work. In E. R. Allgeier & N. B. McCormick (Eds.), *Gender roles and sexual behavior: Changing boundaries.* Palo Alto, Calif.: Mayfield, 1982, in press.

Hall, D. T. A model of coping with role conflict: The role behavior of college educated women. *Administrative Science Quarterly,* 1972, *17,* 471–486.

Helberger, C. Work analysis as a means to achieve equal pay for working women: The Federal Republic of Germany. In R. S. Ratner (Ed.), *Equal employment policy for women: Strategies for implementation in the United States, Canada, and Western Europe.* Philadelphia: Temple University Press, 1980. Pp. 458–483.

Hennig, M., & Jardim, A. *The managerial woman.* New York: Doubleday, 1976.

Herzberg, F., Mausner, B., Peterson, R. A., & Capwell, D. F. *Job attitudes: Review of research and opinion.* Pittsburgh: Psychological Service of Pittsburgh, 1957.

Hoffman, M. L. Maternal employment: 1979. *American Psychologist,* 1979, *34,* 859–865.

Hogan, J. C. *Considerations for preemployment strength testing: Women entering physically demanding jobs.* Washington, D. C.: Advanced Research Resources Organization, May 31, 1979.

Horner, M. S. Toward an understanding of achievement-related conflicts in women. *Journal of Social Issues,* 1972, *28,* 157–175.

Howe, L. K. *Pink collar workers: Inside the world of women's work.* New York: Avon Books, 1977.

Johnson, L. B., & Tangri, S. S. *Results of the national survey of Federal workers by the U. S. Merit Systems Protection Board.* Paper presented as part of the symposium, Sexual harassment at work: Evidence, remedies, and implications. Annual meeting of the American Psychological Association, Los Angeles, August 1981.

Jones, J. E., Jr. The transformation of fair employment practices and policies. In J. P. Goldberg, E. Ahern, W. Haber, & R. A. Oswald (Eds.), *Federal policies and worker status since the thirties.* Madison, Wisconsin: Industrial Relations Research Association, 1976. Pp. 159–207.

Kane, R. D., & Miller, J. Women and apprenticeship: A study of programs designed to facilitate women's participation in the skilled trades. In V. M. Briggs, Jr. & F. F. Foltman (Eds.), *Apprenticeship research: Emerging findings and future trends.* Ithaca, N. Y.: New York State School of Industrial and Labor Relations, Cornell University, 1981. Pp. 83–105.

Kanowitz, L. *Women and the law.* Albuquerque: University of New Mexico Press, 1969.

Kanter, R. M. *Men and women of the corporation.* New York: Basic Books, 1977.

Katzman, D. M. Domestic service: Women's work. In A. H. Stromberg & S. Harkess

(Eds.), *Women working: Theories and facts in perspective*. Palo Alto, Calif.: Mayfield, 1978. Pp. 377–391.

Kay, H. H. *Sex-based discrimination: Text, cases and materials* (2nd ed.). St. Paul: West, 1981.

Kessler-Harris, A. *Women have always worked: A historical overview*. Old Westbury, N. Y.: Feminist Press, 1981.

Kessler-Harris, A. *Out to work: A history of wage-earning women in the United States*. New York: Oxford University Press, 1982.

Koeible, C. E. *An appraisal of machinist-apprenticeship training programs*. Madison: University of Wisconsin Press, 1954.

Kreps, J., & Clark, R. *Sex, age, and work: The changing composition of the labor force*. Baltimore: The Johns Hopkins University Press, 1975.

Kunsh, H. *Apprenticeships in America*. New York: W. W. Norton, 1958.

Lebergott, S. *Manpower in economic growth*. New York: McGraw-Hill, 1964.

Lenny, E. Women's self-confidence in achievement settings. *Psychological Bulletin*, 1977, *84*, 1–13.

Levitan, L. A., Mangum, G. L., & Marshall, R. *Human resources and labor markets* (2nd ed.). New York: Harper & Row, 1976.

Levitan, S. A., Mangum, G. L., & Marshall, R. *Human resources and labor markets* (3rd ed.). New York: Harper & Row, 1981.

MacKinnon, C. A. *Sexual harassment of working women*. New Haven: Yale University Press, 1979.

Magione, T. N. Turnover: Some psychological and demographic correlates. In R. P. Quinn & T. N. Magione (Eds.), *The 1969–1970 survey of working conditions*. Ann Arbor: University of Michigan Survey Research Center, 1973.

Major, B., & Konar, E. *An investigation of sex differences in pay expectations and their possible causes*. Paper presented at Academy of Management meeting, New York, August 1982.

Major, B., & McFarlin, D. *Impression management and gender differences in perceptions of fair performance for pay*. Paper presented at meeting of Midwestern Psychological Association, Minneapolis, May 1982.

Mobley, W. H., Griffith, R. W., Hand, H. H., & Meglino, B. M. Review and conceptual analysis of the employee turnover process. *Psychological Bulletin*, 1979, *86*, 493–522.

Moore, K. A., & Sawhill, I. V. Implications of women's employment for home and family life. In A. H. Stromberg & S. Harkess (Eds.), *Women working: Theories and facts in perspective*. Palo Alto, Calif.: Mayfield, 1978. Pp. 201–225.

Nieva, V. F., & Gutek, B. A. Women's work: What women want, expect, and get. In B. Gutek (Ed.), *New directions for education, work, and careers: Enhancing women's career development*. San Francisco: Jossey-Bass, 1979. Pp. 83–94.

Nieva, V. F., & Gutek, B. A. *Women and work: A psychological perspective*. New York: Praeger, 1981.

O'Farrell, B. Response. In V. M. Briggs, Jr. & F. F. Foltman (Eds.), *Apprenticeship research: Emerging findings and future trends*. Ithaca, N. Y.: New York State School of Industrial and Labor Relations, Cornell University, 1981. Pp. 150–154.

O'Farrell, B., & Harlan, D. *Craftworkers and clerks: The effect of male coworker hostility on women's satisfaction with nontraditional jobs*, working paper No. 62. Wellesley, Massachusetts: Center for Research on Women, 1980.

Office of Personnel Management. *Policy statement on sexual harassment.* January 1980.

O'Leary, V. E. Some attitudinal barriers to occupational aspirations in women. *Psychological Bulletin*, 1974, *81*, 809–826.

Olesen, V. L., & Katsuranis, F. Urban nomads: Women in temporary clerical services. In A. H. Stromberg & S. Harkess (Eds.), *Women working: Theories and facts in perspective*. Palo Alto, Calif.: Mayfield, 1978. Pp. 316–338.

Oppenheimer, V. K. *The female labor force in the United States: Demographic and economic factors governing its growth and changing composition*. Berkeley, Calif.: Institute of International Studies, 1970.

Patterson, M., & Engelberg, L. Women in male-dominated professions. In A. H. Stromberg & S. Harkess (Eds.), *Women working: Theories and facts in perspective*. Palo Alto, Calif.: Mayfield, 1978. Pp. 266–292.

Perlman, R. *On-the-job training in Milwaukee*. Madison: Industrial Relations Research Institute, University of Wisconsin, 1969.

Pleck, J. H. The work-family role system. *Social Problems*, 1977, *24*, 417–427.

Ratner, R. S. Equal employment policy for women: Summary of themes and issues. In R. S. Ratner (Ed.), *Equal employment policy for women: Strategies for implementation in the United States, Canada, and Western Europe*. Philadelphia: Temple University Press, 1980. Pp. 419–440.

Rawalt, M. The "equal rights for men and women amendment" is needed. *Women Lawyers Journal*, 1973, *59*, 4–10.

Remick, H. Beyond equal pay for equal work: Comparable worth in the state of Washington. In R. S. Ratner (Ed.), *Equal employment policy for women: Strategies for implementation in the United States, Canada, and Western Europe*. Philadelphia: Temple University Press, 1980. Pp. 405–419.

Rupp, L. J. *Mobilizing women for war: German and American propaganda, 1939–1945*. Princeton, N. J.: Princeton University Press, 1978.

Smith, R. E. (Ed.), *The subtle revolution: Women at work*. Washington: The Urban Institute, 1979.

Spence, J. T., Deaux, K., & Helmreich, R. L. Sex roles in contemporary American society. In G. Lindzey & E. Aronson (Eds.), *Handbook of social psychology* (3rd ed.). Reading, Mass.: Addison-Wesley, in press.

State of New York, Factory Investigating Commission. *Fourth report of the factory investigating commission*, 1915, *1*, 774.

Stromberg, A. H., & Harkess, S. *Women working: Theories and facts in perspective*. Palo Alto, Calif.: Mayfield, 1978.

Tangri, S. S. *Sexual harassment at work*. Paper presented at the International Interdisciplinary Conference on Women, Haifa, Israel, January 1982.

Temple, Barber, & Sloane, Inc. *Analysis of economic effects of environmental regulations in the integrated iron and steel industry*. Washington, D. C.: U. S. Environmental Protection Agency, July 1977.

The steel industry's tarnished credibility. *Business Week*, December 7, 1981, p. 144.

Ullman, J. C., & Deaux, K. Recent efforts to increase female participation in apprenticeship in the basic steel industry in the Midwest. In V. M. Briggs & F. F. Foltman (Eds.), *Apprenticeship research: Emerging findings and future trends*. Ithaca, N. Y.: New York State School of Industrial and Labor Relations, Cornell University, 1981. Pp. 133–149.

U. S. Council on Wage and Price Stability. *Report to the President on prices and costs in the United States steel industry, 1977*. Washington, D. C.: Council on Wage and Price Stability, October 1977.

U. S. Department of Labor. *Growth of labor law in the United States*. Washington, D. C.: U. S. Government Printing Office, 1967.

U. S. Department of Labor. *Manpower report of the President*. Washington, D. C.: U. S. Government Printing Office, 1971.

U. S. Department of Labor. *Laws on sex discrimination in employment*. Washington, D. C.: U. S. Government Printing Office, 1973.

U. S. Department of Labor. *Employment and training report of the President*. Washington, D. C.: U. S. Government Printing Office, 1976.

U. S. Department of Labor. *Women in traditionally male jobs: The experience of ten public utility companies*. Washington, D. C.: U. S. Government Printing Office, 1978.

U. S. Department of Labor. *Employment and training report of the President*. Washington, D. C.: U. S. Government Printing Office, 1979.

U. S. Department of Labor. *Perspectives on working women: A databook*. Washington, D. C.: U. S. Government Printing Office, 1980.

U. S. Department of Labor. *Employment and earnings*. Washington, D. C.: U. S. Government Printing Office, January 1981.

U. S. Department of Labor. *Employment and unemployment*. Washington, D. C.: U. S. Government Printing Office, April 1981.

U. S. steelmakers slim down from survival. *Business Week*, May 31, 1982, p. 88.

Wall Street Journal, February 12, 1980 (labor letter, p. 1).

Walshok, M. L. *Blue-collar women: Pioneers on the male frontier*. Garden City, N. Y.: Anchor Books, 1981.

Wertheimer, B. M. *We were there: The story of working women in America*. New York: Pantheon, 1977.

Index

ABOUT THE AUTHORS

KAY DEAUX is Professor of Psychology at Purdue University. During the 1983–84 academic year, she is a Fellow at the Center for Advanced Studies in the Behavioral Sciences in Stanford, California.

Dr. Deaux has published widely in the areas of social psychology, specializing in topics of sex roles and women. She authored *The Behavior of Women and Men* and coauthored (with Lawrence Wrightsman) *Social Psychology in the 80s*. Dr. Deaux received her B.A. from Northwestern University and her Ph.D. from the University of Texas at Austin.

JOSEPH C. ULLMAN is Program Director and Professor of Management in the College of Business Administration, University of South Carolina. Previously he was Professor of Management and Director of the Center for Public Policy and Public Administration at Purdue University.

Dr. Ullman is interested in the operation and evaluation of human resource programs in the employment area. He received his B.A. from Northwestern University and his Ph.D. from the University of Chicago.

G